Exodus:
Called for Redemptive Mission

Page H. Kelley

CONVENTION PRESS ● Nashville, Tennessee

5132-23

This book is the text for a course in the subject area Bible
Studies of the Church Study Course.
Target group: This book is designed for adults and is part of the
Church Study Course offerings. The 1963 statement of "The
Baptist Faith and Message" is the doctrinal guideline for the
writer and editor.

Dewey Decimal Classification Number: 222.12
Printed in the United States of America

Contents

A Word for Beginning . . .

A new breed of nomads wanders over the face of the earth. These are the migrant workers, the war refugees, the military personnel, the hard-core unemployed, and the job transferees.
. . . Does Exodus have anything to say to our situation?

So writes Dr. Page H. Kelley, author of this book. His question is answered in the affirmative; the answer is on every page. Out of his experience as Professor of Old Testament Interpretation at The Southern Baptist Theological Seminary, Louisville, Kentucky, his speaking and teaching in the churches, and his experience as missionary serving in South America, Dr. Kelley writes with conviction and authority.

The author reminds us that Exodus tells how Abraham's seed, through God's deliverance from Egypt, became the nation Israel. That is to say, Israel first knew God as Redeemer. Thus the reader is clued into the study very early by linking his own knowledge of God as Redeemer with Israel's. Exodus is Israel's redemption story.

This January Bible Study, then, provides the members of the churches and others with a Bible study which has both information and inspiration. It should be a good beginning for the two-year Bold Mission emphasis in our denomination for 1977-78.

The book can be used in either personal or group study. In both uses the personal learning activities at the end of each chapter will help the learner review and fix the material covered. When study is done in a group, the companion teaching guide and study guide will supply helpful resources to teacher and member. Guidance for use of the personal learning activities in this textbook will be found in the section headed "The Church Study Course" at the back of the book. The commentary is based on the Revised Standard Version text unless otherwise indicated.

Also at the very back of the book is a Church Study Course Credit Request (Form 151). Upon completion of this book study the pupil should mail in the completed form to the address indicated. Two copies of the credit award will be mailed to the applicant's church—one for the church's record, the other for the pupil's own use.

Ralph L. Murray, editor.

1

An Oppressed People

Exodus 1:1 to 2:25

1. The Significance of the Exodus

Few events in history have had such far-reaching effects as Israel's Exodus out of Egypt. The Exodus event lies at the very heart of the Old Testament. The Exodus is to the Old Covenant what the resurrection is to the New.

Israel herself regarded the Exodus as the most significant event in her history. Across the centuries this mighty act of God was confessed by her people (Deut. 6:20-25; 26:5-9; Josh. 24:5-7). It was preached by her prophets (Hos. 11:1; Amos 3:1-2; Mic. 6:3-5). It was sung by her poets (Pss. 77:11-20; 78; 105:26-45; 106; 114; 135; 136). And it was celebrated in the Passover, the best loved of all her sacrificial feasts. Through this event such words as "redemption" and "salvation" first entered her religious vocabulary.

The Exodus has continued to fascinate men down to our own day. It has inspired musicians, painters, sculptors, writers, and film producers. One has only to think of Handel's oratorio *Israel in Egypt* or Michelangelo's sculpture of Moses to discover the truth of that statement. Moses in his ark of bulrushes, the burning bush, and the crossing of the sea are among the scenes from the Exodus that have been painted by artists from many lands. The Negro slaves in the cotton fields of the South felt a kinship with the ancient Israelites in Egypt. Out of their bondage came such spirituals as "Go Down, Moses." In more recent times movie producers have tried to capture Moses and the Israelites in film epics and to bring alive their story on the screen. It is safe to say that no other event in Old Testament times has inspired so much music, art, or literature as has the Exodus.

Of course the greatest effect of the Exodus was upon Israel itself. Through this unforgettable experience the nation had its rebirth. Prior to this the Israelites had lived as loosely related clans without any sense of national unity. It was the Exodus followed by the covenant of Sinai that welded them together and marked the beginning of their nationhood.

This means that the study of Israelite history properly ought to begin with the study of the Exodus. Abraham's seed, through God's deliverance from Egypt, became the nation Israel. That is to say, Israel first knew God as Redeemer. The events recorded in Genesis serve as a prologue to those found in Exodus. The Genesis account records the promise of land and descendants first made to Abraham (Gen. 12:1-3) and later repeated to Isaac (Gen. 26:3-4) and to Jacob (Gen. 28:13-14).

It was no accident that when God appeared to Moses at the burning bush he said, " 'I am the God of your father, the God of Abraham, the God of Isaac, and the God of Jacob' " (Ex. 3:6). This covenant-keeping God had not forgotten the promise made to the fathers. He had seen the affliction of his people. He had heard their cry of distress. And now he was sending Moses to deliver them from their bondage and to bring them at last to their promised home. God's faithfulness to his promise is the golden thread that binds these accounts together.

The Exodus is significant for another reason. It is that it emphasizes the mystery of divine election. The whole subject of election has stirred up considerable discussion. Why should God elect a slave people to receive his revelation rather than some mighty nation like Egypt or Babylon? Some have interpreted Israel's faith in her election as nothing more than racial and religious pride on her part. Some Israelites doubtlessly were guilty of such an attitude. The Talmud[1] records a legend that God at first offered his revelation to all the nations. But when they heard its contents, they refused to accept it. It was then offered to Israel, and she accepted it. This ancient legend is an attempt to clear God of the charge of favoritism.

The Old Testament itself warns Israel against pride in her election. It solemnly reminds her that God did not choose her because of any inherent strength or goodness on her part (Deut. 7:6-8; 9:4-6). Her call and election came by grace alone. Furthermore, election brought her no comfortable special status. Rather, being called of God exposed her to greater hardships, to greater trials, and to greater sacrifices than other nations had to face.

The call to be a Christian also is like this. Our election bestows on us a great honor but also a great obligation. We are elected not so much to privilege as to service. We often fail to communicate this in our preaching and in our living. How hard it is for us to take Jesus' words seriously! He said, " 'Whoever does not bear his own cross and come after me, cannot be my disciple' " (Luke 14:27). It was Dietrich Bonhoeffer who said, "When Christ calls a man, he bids him come and die."[2]

A further reason for the significance of the Exodus is that it stresses the importance of human freedom. There was something unique about Israel's beginning as a nation. It was that she was a nation of freed men who had been liberated from bondage. No other nation in ancient times is known to have had such a beginning. And the fact that the Israelites were former slaves caused them to value their freedom as a gift from God and to guard it zealously. Never again would they be content to be in bondage to any man or nation. Often they would be called upon to defend their freedom. Often they would lose it for a while. But the ideal of freedom never died. Later generations learned to pray, " 'This year Jews are enslaved; may next year set them free.' "[3]

Because of Israel's experience in Egypt her ethical concepts were changed. A deep-seated and fundamental bias was introduced into the ethical teachings of the Old Testament. It was a bias in favor of the weak, the downtrodden, and the oppressed. God came to be understood as the champion and defender of the defenseless members of society—the foreigner, the widow, the orphan, and the slave. The Old Testament is extremely suspicious of those who grow powerful and wealthy in the midst of weakness and poverty. Through the Exodus experience the foundation was laid for the preaching of the great prophets. Their hallmark was the demand for justice and righteousness in human society.

The story of the Exodus is not one that a nation would have invented about itself. From beginning to end it glorifies God at the expense of Israel. God chose a weak, dispirited slave people whom the justice of the world had passed by. For them there was no protecting law. Their only claim on God's mercy was their misfortune and their deep need of him. False gods would have chosen the strong and the wealthy. These could have repaid them with magnificent temples and generous offerings. But God chose a people who were not a people—just a motley crew of slaves—to carry his message and to bless the world. Truly his ways are past finding out! (See Rom. 11:33, KJV.)

Paul wrote in 1 Corinthians 10:11, "These things happened to them as a warning, but they were written down for our instruction." He was referring primarily to the story of the golden calf in Exodus 32. But his words have a broader application. In a real sense everything in the book of Exodus was written for our instruction. This book belongs to that larger treasure of Scripture which is said to be "profitable for teaching, for reproof, for correction, and for training in righteousness, that the man of God may be complete, equipped for every good work" (2 Tim. 3:16-17).

2. The Bondage of the Hebrews *(1:1-14)*

The opening verses of chapter 1 are a bridge between Genesis and Exodus. They list the twelve sons of Jacob who fled to Egypt to escape famine. Then they tell how Joseph and his brothers and all that generation died in Egypt, but how their descendants multiplied greatly and filled the land. These verses mark the transition from the family history of the patriarchs to the national history of Israel. From this point onward in Exodus the division into tribes is almost completely ignored. The story is concerned with Israel as a national unity.

The multiplication of the Israelites led to their being regarded as aliens. They began to be looked upon with fear and distrust, especially when there arose a new king who did not know Joseph (v. 8). This means that the new king did not remember Joseph. Therefore he did not feel any obligation to the Israelites because of what Joseph had done for Egypt.

We are not told how long the Israelites had been in Egypt when the attitude toward them changed. Neither are we told the name of the king responsible for this new policy. To find out who he was and when he lived, we must piece together the clues provided by the Bible and by archaeology.

According to Exodus 12:40, the Israelites were in Egypt a total of 430 years. It is thought by many that Joseph rose to power in Egypt under the Hyksos. These were foreign rulers of Semitic origin who swept out of the north and invaded Egypt shortly after 1700 B.C. Armed with a new weapon, the horse-drawn chariot, they conquered all the lands that lay in their path. They remained in power until they were driven out by a native Egyptian ruler around 1550 B.C.

That Joseph entered Egypt early in the Hyksos period seems highly likely. He was also of Semitic origin and would have been looked upon with favor. The conditions were right for him to rise to power and for his father and brothers to be warmly received when they arrived in Egypt.

There is further evidence bearing on this subject in Exodus 1:11. There we learn that the Israelite laborers were forced to build the store-cities of Pithom and Raamses. Archaeology has shown that these two cities were built during the reigns of Sethos I (1305-1290 B.C.) and Ramses II (1290-1224 B.C.). On the basis of this evidence John Bright and other Old Testament scholars have concluded that the Exodus took place around 1250 B.C.[4] This would make Sethos I the pharaoh who began the oppression of Israel and Ramses II the pharaoh of the Exodus.

Let us return for a moment to the statement of Exodus 12:40. There we learn that the Israelites were in Egypt a total of 430 years. Dating the Exodus around 1250 B.C. would place the beginning of their sojourn in Egypt shortly after 1700 B.C. And this was precisely the time when the Hyksos were beginning their rule in Egypt. This fact, plus other archaeological evidence, firmly supports a thirteenth-century date for the Exodus. In this event the king who did not know Joseph probably was Sethos I.

Pharaoh tried to stop the Israelites from multiplying by compelling them to do slave labor. He placed taskmasters over them and set them to work building his store-cities. But the more they were oppressed the more they multiplied. This was the beginning of a contest between the king of Egypt and the King of the universe, and in such a contest the king of Egypt was bound to lose.

3. Pharaoh's Command to the Midwives *(1:15-22)*

Having failed to stop the growth of the Israelites through forced labor, Pharaoh tried a harsher method. There were two Hebrew midwives who attended the Hebrew women during childbirth. One was named Shiphrah, meaning "beauty" or "fair one." The other was named Puah, perhaps meaning "splendid one." Pharaoh summoned these two and commanded them to watch the Hebrew women when they were upon the birthstool. The birthstool consisted of two stone discs like those of a potter's wheel. Egyptian records tell how women sat or kneeled upon such stones at the time of delivery. The midwives were commanded to kill all the sons born to the Hebrews but to spare their daughters. The killing of the sons in time would have wiped out the Hebrew people. Their daughters then would have become slave wives of the Egyptian men.

But the two Hebrew midwives outsmarted Pharaoh. Because they feared God, they let the male children live. There is a touch of humor in their explanation to Pharaoh about what had happened. Hebrew women were just so lively that they gave birth before the midwives had time to reach them! There was no way then for them to carry out Pharaoh's command.

But Pharaoh was not to be outdone. He gave a direct command to all his people. It was that every newborn son of the Hebrews be thrown into the Nile. With this command his campaign to wipe out the Israelites had reached its height. All Egypt had been recruited to stop the population explosion of the enemy. And with this command the stage was set for the birth of Moses.

4. The Birth of Moses *(2:1-10)*

The story of God and his people in the Old Testament has three new sections, each with an important introduction. The first is the beginning of the patriarchal history (Gen. 12). The second is the beginning of the nation's history (Ex. 1). The third is the begiming of the history of the kings (1 Sam. 1). At each of these pivotal points in the story there is a long birth narrative. The patriarchal history opens with the story of Isaac's birth. The nation's history begins with the birth of Moses. And the history of the kings is prefaced by the account of Samuel's birth. There is more to this than meets the eye, for all of God's great works in history begin with the birth of a child.

The beginning of the New Testament marks still another pivotal point in the continuing story of God and his people. And it too is marked by a birth narrative. Once again there is heard a mother's prayer and a baby's cry. The important difference is that this child was born to be King of kings and Lord of lords. Moses was born to deliver Israel from the bondage of Egypt, but Jesus came to save his people from their sins. He dealt with a greater bondage and effected a far greater deliverance.

Pharaoh had issued a decree that every newborn son of Israelites was to be destroyed by drowning. Then Moses was born. His parents belonged to the tribe of Levi (2:1), and we are told later that their names were Amram and Jochebed (6:20). This child was to slip through Pharaoh's net and become the deliverer of God's people.

At first the mother tried to hide her baby from the Egyptian authorities. For three months she was successful. But Moses was a healthy baby, and his mother knew that she could not hide him indefinitely. So she devised a plan for saving him. She built an ark of bulrushes, a word used to designate the stalks of the papyrus plant. The story tells of the great care she took to prevent its leaking; she sealed it with pitch. She even placed a cover on it, for Pharaoh's daughter later had to open it to remove the baby (v.6).

The Hebrew word for ark is *tebah*. It occurs elsewhere only in the story of Noah's ark (Gen. 6:14). A different word is used for the ark of the covenant (Ex. 25:10). It is significant that both Noah and Moses were saved from drowning by means of an ark. And each of them was delivered in order that he might deliver others. Noah saved his family in order that the human race might have a new beginning. And Moses delivered the Chosen People in order that they might have a new beginning in the Promised Land.

There is no mention of God in the story of Moses' rescue from death. And yet it is clear that he was working through these events to perform a miracle. Moses was placed in the ark and set adrift on the waters of the Nile. Miriam, his sister, was stationed nearby to see what would become of him. At this point Pharaoh's daughter entered the picture. She and her maidens had come to bathe in the Nile. Then she spied the small ark and sent one of her maidens to fetch it. Opening the cover to the ark, she discovered the small baby, recognized him as one of the despised Hebrews, and yet had pity on him. She could just as easily have signed his death warrant. Surely God was guiding the course of these events.

One of the delightful features of this story is the part played by Moses' sister. She volunteered her services to Pharaoh's daughter to find a Hebrew woman to nurse the child. And to whom should she turn but the child's own mother? And so Jochebed got her child back, at least for a while. She nursed the child until he was old enough to be weaned and to become the adopted son of the Egyptian princess. It is interesting to note that those who played a part in this drama of deliverance were all women—the midwives, Jochebed, Miriam, Pharaoh's daughter, and her maidens.

In the Bible children are usually named directly after their birth. Here, however, the name is given only after the child has been weaned and has come under the care of Pharaoh's daughter. She named him Moses because she had drawn him out of the water. The Hebrew word meaning "to draw out" is similar in sound to the word Moses. However, it is generally recognized that Moses is an Egyptian name and that its Egyptian meaning is "born of" or "son of." (Thus Tutmoses, the name of a famous Egyptian ruler, means "Son of Tut.") The Egyptian origin of Moses' name is further evidence of the historical reliability of the Exodus account.

The story of Moses' birth and miraculous rescue illustrates the divine wisdom and power. The point of the story is that God overrules

the evil designs of all who would oppose him. Who would have imag-
ined that the child whose death had been decreed by Pharaoh would
grow up as a prince in Pharaoh's own house? The men of the Bible
know that although evil men may have plenty of rope, the end of the
rope is always in God's hands.

5. Moses' Murder of an Egyptian *(2:11-15)*

There is a considerable lapse of time between verses 10 and 11. The
text in verse 11 presents Moses as a grown man. According to Acts
7:23, he was forty years of age when these events took place. We know
little about what had happened to him during the interval since his
rescue from the Nile. Presumably he had continued to live in Pharaoh's
palace. Acts 7:22 informs us that he was instructed in all the wisdom of
the Egyptians. He must have come to resemble an Egyptian in every
way, for he was later mistaken for one (Ex. 2:19).

Moses had been spared the hardships of the slavery of the Hebrews.
However, through some means unknown to us, he had become aware
that he really belonged to them. A later writer interprets Moses' identification with his brethren as a conscious decision on his part. "By
faith Moses, when he was grown up, refused to be called the son of
Pharaoh's daughter, choosing rather to share ill-treatment with the people of God than to enjoy the fleeting pleasures of sin" (Heb. 11:24-25).

Events came to a climax when Moses was out walking in the field
one day. By some hidden instinct he was drawn to seek out his
brethren. "He went out to his people and looked on their burdens" (v.
11). This means that he felt compassion for them and was grieved at
their burdens.

But on that fateful day Moses' compassion was translated into action. He saw an Egyptian taskmaster strike a Hebrew slave. Righteous
indignation flamed up in his heart. However, he was anxious that any
action on his part be done in secrecy. He looked this way and that to
make sure no one was looking. Then he leaped upon the offender and
killed him. He quickly dug a grave in the sand and buried his victim
where he supposed he would never be found.

On the following day Moses returned to his Hebrew brethren and to
his surprise found two of them fighting each other. One was the obvious
aggressor. The text speaks of him as the one "that did the wrong" (v.
13). Moses tried to intervene on behalf of the weaker of the two. His
concern was that justice be done. However, the Hebrew who was bully-
ing his brother rudely rejected Moses' intervention. He also challenged
Moses' authority to act as mediator. He misinterpreted Moses' motive.

Acts 7:25 says that Moses "supposed that his brethren understood that God was giving them deliverance by his hand, but they did not understand." The offending Hebrew not only challenged Moses' authority, but he also let it be known that he was aware of what had taken place on the previous day. He said, "Who made you a prince and a judge over us? Do you mean to kill me as you killed the Egyptian?' " (v. 14). Apparently the man whom Moses had saved from the Egyptian the day before had told what had happened.

Moses' intervention was certainly a high-handed act. He had acted entirely on his own initiative and without any authority. Now his secret was out, and it was being used as a weapon against him. He was afraid, and with good reason. When Pharaoh heard what had happened, he sought to kill Moses. Moses had not acted in obedience to a command from God, for God had not yet spoken to him. In fact, there is no word of commendation or reassurance from God after the incident. Moses was forced to flee like a common criminal and seek asylum in the desert. Furthermore, forty years passed before God was ready to send him back to Egypt (Ex. 7:7).

Moses' murder of the Egyptian and his attempt to mediate between his quarreling brethren underscore certain of his character traits. One is his readiness to identify himself with his people. Another is his blazing anger at the sight of wrong and his passionate desire for justice. Also evident here is Moses' willingess to thrust himself into difficult situations in order to serve as mediator. A further trait revealed here is his tendency to act hastily and with a heavy hand. It was this last trait that kept him in trouble during much of his ministry and seems to have prevented his entering the land of Canaan.

Moses failed at first partly because he was betrayed by his own kind. His fellow Hebrews rejected both his authority and his demand for justice. Moses' rejection reminds us of that of Jesus. It was true of both of these that when they came to their own, their own received them not (John 1:11).

6. Moses' Flight to Midian *(2:16-25)*

When Moses fled from Pharaoh, he went to dwell in the land of Midian (2:15). The Old Testament represents the Midianites as bedouin tribesmen of the desert regions to the south and east of Palestine. According to Genesis 25:1-2 Midian was the son of Abraham by his wife Keturah. The Midianites therefore were regarded as distantly related to the Israelites. Midianite traders are reported to have sold Joseph into Egypt (Gen. 37:28). The Midianites were famous for their camels (Judg.

7:12; Isa. 60:6). With the aid of these camels they were able to travel at great speed and to surprise their neighbors with sudden raids (Judg. 6:1-6). The crushing defeat which Gideon inflicted on the Midianites in the valley of Jezreel (Judg. 7) was long remembered in history as "the day of Midian" (Isa. 9:4). The fact that the Israelites and Midianites are often pictured as being at war with each other makes Moses' peaceful association with a group of them all the more remarkable. It is probable that we are dealing here with an earlier relationship than that recorded in Judges.

One day after he had arrived in the land of Midian, Moses sat down beside a well. It is noteworthy how often wells play a part in biblical stories. Because of scanty rainfall wells were of great importance, especially for the watering of flocks and herds. Nomadic tribes often fought over the possession of a well (Gen. 21:25-31; 26:18-22). It was a social event when shepherds gathered at a well to water their flocks. Wells were usually covered over with a large flat stone to prevent animals' falling into them (Ex. 21:33). Sometimes a stone was so big and heavy that women coming to draw water could not lift it (Gen. 29:2-10). One of Jesus' most memorable conversations was with a Samaritan woman who had come to draw water from Jacob's well (John 4).

As Moses waited beside the well, seven daughters of the priest of Midian came to water their father's flock. Other shepherds were also pasturing their flocks nearby. They tried to take advantage of the women. The shepherds waited until these women had labored to fill the troughs with water. The shepherds then drove the women away and led their own flocks to the watering troughs.

Once again it was Moses to the rescue. His sense of justice would not permit him to see the women mistreated. Perhaps most of his contemporaries thought of women as having no rights, but he did not share this view. He stood up for them and helped them water their flock. Moses was never slow to take a stand against injustice and oppression, no matter who the victim might be.

The priest of Midian was surprised when his daughters got home, because it was earlier in the day than usual. Apparently, they were often harassed by the shepherds. When he asked for an explanation, they said, " 'An Egyptian delivered us out of the hand of the shepherds, and even drew water for us and watered the flock' " (2:19). The priest then scolded his daughters for not inviting the friendly stranger to come home with them for a meal. The custom of hospitality of the desert demanded that they do this. They had shown rudeness and a lack of appreciation in leaving Moses beside the well.

Their oversight was soon corrected. An invitation to dinner was sent to Moses, and he accepted. His own people had rejected him, but in the tent of a Midianite he found hospitality. He also found a wife. The priest's daughter Zipporah was given to him in marriage. She bore him a son, whom Moses named Gershom. The name he gave his newborn son indicated that Moses did not consider Midian to be his permanent home. Gershom means "a stranger there." It was as if Moses knew that his stay there would be temporary.

There is some confusion about the name of Moses' father-in-law. In 2:18 he is called Reuel. However, in 3:1 he is called Jethro. In Judges 4:11 he is called Hobab the Kenite. To complicate matters still further, in Numbers 10:29 both Hobab and Reuel are mentioned and one of them is said to be Moses' father-in-law. However, the Hebrew text does not make clear whether the father-in-law is Hobab or Reuel. If it is Reuel, then Hobab is Moses' brother-in-law, and this is the way it is interpreted in *The New English Bible.* A reasonable solution seems to be that Moses' father-in-law was known both as Reuel and as Jethro, and that Hobab was his son. Therefore Hobab was Moses' brother-in-law. However, since other interpretations are possible, one must not be dogmatic.

Chapter 2 ends with a hopeful note. It is that the Egyptian king who had begun the persecution of the Israelites was dead. This king was Sethos I, and the year of his death was 1290 B.C.. In the meantime the oppression of the Israelites continued unabated under Ramses II (1290-1224 B.C.), the successor to Sethos I. Kings might change, but their policies remained the same.

In the bitterness of their bondage the Israelites cried out for help, and their cry came up to God (2:23). Verbs are piled up in these verses to show that God is the God of love and compassion. "God heard . . . God remembered . . . God saw . . . and God knew" (2:24-25). The reader is made aware that something significant is about to take place. What will it be? How will God deliver his people from their oppression? Who will be the instrument of the deliverance? These questions will be answered in the account of the call and commission of Moses and the events that follow.

7. Lessons for Life from the Scriptures

The story of the bondage of the Israelites and of the birth and early life of Moses contains some valuable lessons for us.

God's call and election are by grace alone. How odd that God should choose a nation of slaves to be his people! If we demand a reason for God's love for Israel, the simplest is this: God loved Israel because God loved Israel. In other words, the root and ground of God's love lay in him and not in them. And so it is with us. Jesus said, " 'You did not choose me, but I chose you' " (John 15:16). John wrote that the essence of love is found not in our love for God but in his love for us (1 John 4:10).

God's call and election are to sacrificial service. Israel's election did not guarantee her earthly success and an easy trip to heaven. Rather, her call and election exposed her to greater hardships and to greater sacrifices than other nations had to face. Even so we are called to take up our cross and follow Jesus to Calvary. No man can be raised with Christ who has not also died with him.

Human freedom is of great value in the sight of God. Of course God is concerned that men should be freed from the bondage of sin. For this cause he sent his own Son to die on the cross. But God is also concerned that men should be liberated from all forms of bondage—physical as well as spiritual. All men are created in the image of God and are of infinite value in his sight. Exodus teaches us that God takes a special interest in those who have been robbed of their rights. Jesus also demonstrated in his ministry such an interest. He was concerned with social and religious outcasts, with the poor and lowly, and with the downtrodden of his day. And he taught that when we render service to persons like this we render service to him. (Matt. 25:31-46).

Across the centuries tyrants have built their empires with the lifeblood of the suffering masses. Oppression is still alive in many parts of the world. Multitudes are denied their freedom and dignity as human beings. Christians should never condone any system that treats a fellow human being as nothing but a commodity in the labor market, a thing to be exploited.

God works out his will for our lives in mysterious ways. Moses' sojourn in the land of Midian probably seemed to him like a senseless waste of time. But God in his wisdom was training Moses in the rigors of desert living so that he could lead the Israelites through this same desert. God sometimes leads us on what seems to be a detour in our spiritual pilgrimage. Later, however, we look back and realize that what seemed at the time to be a detour was in fact the most important part of the journey. Moses might never have had his vision at the burning bush had he not been forced to flee to Midian. God works all things together for good to those who are called according to his purpose (Rom. 8:28).

----

¹Talmud: The authoritative body of Jewish tradition comprising the Mishnah and Gemara. (Mishnah: the body of Jewish law supplementing the Scriptural law and forming the legal part of the Talmud. The Mishnah was compiled about A.D. 200 and made the basic part of the Talmud. Gemara: A commentary on the Mishnah forming the second part of the Talmud.)

²Dietrich Bonhoeffer, *The Cost of Discipleship* (New York: The Macmillan Company, 1959), p. 79.

³From *The Book of Exodus*, A Critical Theological Commentary, by Brevard S. Childs. The Westminster Press. Copyright © 1974, Brevard S. Childs. Used by permission.

⁴John Bright, *A History of Israel*, 2nd ed. (Philadelphia: The Westminster Press, 1972), p. 121.

Personal Learning Activities

1. The Exodus is significant because (choose correct responses):
   ____ (1) Through it Israel was born as a nation.
   ____ (2) It emphasizes the mystery of divine election.
   ____ (3) It marks Israel as a favored people.
   ____ (4) It stresses the importance of human freedom.
   ____ (5) It helps date Old Testament writings.
2. The date of the Exodus, according to Dr. Kelly, was (choose one):
   ____ (1) 1700 B.C.
   ____ (2) 430 B.C.
   ____ (3) 1250 B.C.
3. The pharaoh of the Exodus was probably (choose one):
   ____ (1) Hyksos.
   ____ (2) Ramses II.
   ____ (3) Sethos I.
4. Four periods in God's relation to his people as recorded in the Bible begin with a birth narrative. The persons whose births are recorded are (choose four):
   ____ (1) Isaac (patriarchs).   ____ (4) Samuel (kings).
   ____ (2) Moses (Exodus).   ____ (5) Isaiah (prophets).
   ____ (3) Gideon (judges).   ____ (6) Jesus (the new covenant).

Answers:
1. (1), (2), (4); 2. (3); 3. (2); 4. (1), (2), (4), (6).

2

God's Call and Man's Response

Exodus 3:1 to 4:31

In our previous study we saw that God heard the cry of his oppressed people and came down to help them (Ex. 2:23-25). The God of the Old Testament is not removed from the sufferings of people. He is near at hand to all who call on him. His nearness and his readiness to help are two of the qualities that distinguish him from false gods. He is the Redeemer God, the friend of the oppressed, the God who acts.

When God acts, however, he acts through the instrumentality of people. And when God needs a person for his service, he knows where to find one. He had determined to free Israel from the bondage of Egypt, and he chose to work through a man who had been providentially trained for the task. Moses had not only been trained in Pharaoh's court but he also had been schooled in the rigors of desert living for forty years. God had been watching over him from the very beginning to prepare him for his task.

1. The Nature of God's Call

Call narratives are a vital part of the Old Testament record. In addition to the call of Moses we read how God called such men as Abraham (Gen. 12:1-3), Gideon (Judg. 6:11-40), and Saul (1 Sam. 9:1 to 10:13). There are also accounts of the calls of various prophets. These include Isaiah (Isa. 6:1-8), Jeremiah (Jer. 1:4-10), and Ezekiel (Ezek. 1:1 to 3:15). In the New Testament the most dramatic call experience is that of Paul (Acts 9:1-19).

Several features of these call experiences deserve attention. One is the coupling of the divine call with a vision of God. Isaiah saw a vision of God seated upon an exalted throne and surrounded by heavenly creatures called seraphim (Isa. 6:1-4). Ezekiel saw the glory of the Lord riding upon a chariot and carried about by four living creatures (Ezek. 1:4-28). Moses was following his father-in-law's flock in the wilderness when he came upon an astonishing sight. Before his very eyes he saw a bush, burning but not consumed by the flames. And turning aside to see the bush, he experienced an encounter with God.

A second feature of the call experiences of the Old Testament is their emphasis on the spoken command of God. What the one who is called of God *sees* is not nearly so important as what he *hears*. The vision of God is given not for one's private enjoyment but in order that he may be sent to serve. Abraham heard God saying, " 'Go from your country and your kindred and I will make of you . . . a blessing' " (Gen. 12:1-2). Isaiah heard the inescapable command, " 'Go. . . . Until cities lie waste without inhabitant . . . and the land is utterly desolate' " (Isa. 6:9,11). Ezekiel was told, " 'Son of man, I have made you a watchman for the house of Israel' " (Ezek. 33:7). And upon the astonished ears of Moses fell the command, " 'Come, I will send you to Pharaoh that you may bring forth my people . . . out of Egypt' " (Ex. 3:10).

A third feature of these accounts is the variety of ways in which those who were called made their responses. The responses fall into two main categories. Some accepted the divine call in a spirit of submission and at times even with enthusiasm. Isaiah and Ezekiel belong to this class. Isaiah volunteered to be sent on divine mission even before he understood what that mission would involve. God had taken care of his past and could have his future. Ezekiel likewise responded positively to his call. The word of God he was called to proclaim was in his mouth "as sweet as honey" (Ezek. 3:3).

It was not so with such men as Moses, Gideon, Saul, and Jeremiah. Gideon had to be doubly sure that God had really called him to deliver Israel from the Midianites. He felt totally inadequate for such a task. He expressed his reluctance in these words, " 'Pray, Lord, how can I deliver Israel? Behold, my clan is the weakest in Manasseh, and I am the least in my family' " (Judg. 6:15). He also tested the validity of God's command by putting out the fleece (Judg. 6:36-40. Saul protested his inadequacy when called to be king over Israel. He exclaimed, " 'Am I not a Benjaminite, from the least of the tribes of Israel? And is not my family the humblest of all the families of the tribe of Benjamin?' " (1 Sam. 9:21). When the people assembled to make him king, he was so bashful that he hid himself among the baggage (1 Sam.

10:22). Among the prophets Jeremiah was the most reluctant. Faced with the call of God he cried out, " 'Ah, Lord God! Behold, I do not know how to speak, for I am only a youth' " (Jer. 1:6). More resistant to the divine call than any of the others, however, was Moses. In fact, he seems to have been the first to adopt such an attitude, which is often dubbed "the Moses complex." Before his defenses were shattered, he had offered a fivefold argument against following God's call. His excuses and God's response to them will be examined in greater detail below.

A fourth feature of the call accounts in the Old Testament is the forewarning of rejection woven into them. This is especially true in the case of Moses and the prophets. God never minimizes the cost of discipleship in order to get men to follow him. One committed disciple is worth more than a hundred half-hearted ones. Jesus urged those who follow him to count the cost at the beginning of the course so that they would not falter in the middle (Luke 14:25-33). Isaiah was told that his preaching would only result in making the hearts of his people fat, their ears heavy, and their eyes shut (Isa. 6:10). Jeremiah was called to be an adversary to the whole land of Judah—its kings, its princes, its priests, and its people (Jer. 1:18-19). Moses was sent to Pharaoh, but he was warned beforehand that the king would harden his heart and refuse to let the people go (Ex. 4:21).

A fifth element in the call accounts of the Old Testament is the assurance of the divine presence. The supreme promise that God makes to those who follow him is, "I will be with you." To the protesting Moses he said, " 'But I will be with you; and this shall be the sign that I have sent you' " (Ex. 3:12). To Joshua he said, " 'As I was with Moses, so I will be with you; I will not fail you or forsake you' " (Josh. 1:5). Jeremiah was given this reassuring promise, " 'Be not afraid of them, for I am with you to deliver you, says the Lord' " (Jer. 1:8). Jesus ended the Great Commission with the promise, " 'Lo, I am with you always, to the close of the age' " (Matt. 28:20).

Those who hear and respond to the call of God are never promised an easy life. They are not promised success or the comforts that other men highly treasure. Rather, they are promised reproach and misunderstanding and a cross. But they are also promised a blessed life of intimate fellowship with the heavenly Father. They are promised that even when they walk through dark valleys, they will still have his presence. And such a promise is all that they ask or expect. No mountain is too high, no river too deep, no desert too dry, but that they are able to conquer in his name.

2. The Burning Bush (3:1-6)

Having fled from Egypt, Moses married the daughter of Jethro, the priest of Midian. His marriage contract apparently required that he tend the flocks of his father-in-law. The life of a shepherd is a lonely one. Moses had abundant time for meditation and reflection. One thought must have been uppermost in his mind. It was the memory of the suffering of his brethren in Egypt. He wanted to help them, but how could he do so when he was so far away?

One day the answer came. He had led Jethro's flock to the west side of the desert, to the mountain of God (v. 1). This mountain is sometimes called Horeb and sometimes Sinai. Just where it was located we are not certain. Some archaeologists would place it in the northern part of the Sinai peninsula near Kadesh. Others, convinced that it was a volcanic mountain, have located it in northwest Arabia, east of the Gulf of Aqaba. However, the traditional site is in the southern part of the Sinai peninsula. Since early Christian times it has been identified with *Jebel Musa,* an Arabic meaning "Mountain of Moses." This seems to be the most likely location of all that have been proposed.

As Moses led his flock near the sacred mountain, he saw a strange sight. A bush was burning, but was not consumed by the flames. The Hebrew word for bush *(seneh)* is similar in sound to the name Sinai. The author no doubt selected the word for this reason. It occurs elsewhere only in Deuteronomy 33:16, where the Lord is referred to as "him that dwelt in the bush."

The bush is usually identified as a thorn bush or a blackberry bush. However, no positive identification can be made. None is needed. Neither do we need to waste time speculating about what made the bush burn without being consumed. It is enough to recognize that Moses saw it as "a great sight" (v. 3). He decided to go over and take a closer look.

Little did Moses realize what a revolution was about to take place. What began as just another day in his life turned out to be an absolutely new experience for him. His vision at the burning bush marked the end of his life as a shepherd and the beginning of his life as a deliverer.

As Moses approached the bush, God called his name and he answered, " 'Here am I' " (3:4). His response meant that he was ready to listen and to obey. However, he was not yet aware of the overwhelming nature of the task about to be assigned to him. Moses was told to put off his shoes from his feet since the place where he was standing was holy ground. (Moslems still observe the custom of removing their shoes when they enter a sanctuary.)

God appeared to Moses not as a new God, but as the God of the fathers, " 'the God of Abraham, the God of Isaac, and the God of Jacob' " (v. 6). His promises to the fathers had not been forgotten. They were now to be fulfilled through the Exodus. At this awesome revelation of God, Moses hid his face, for he was afraid to look at God.

3. The Commission of Moses *(3:7-12)*

In this conversation between God and Moses three things are made clear. The first is God's firm resolution to rescue his people from their affliction. The second is his choice of Moses to be their deliverer. And the third is the growing reluctance of Moses to undertake such a difficult task.

God's determination to rescue his people from bondage is described in verses 7-8. One of the outstanding characteristics of Moses' God is that he does not sit comfortably in heaven, but enters the struggles of earth. In his concern for Israel he was very much like Moses himself. He too had been listening to the cry of his people and had decided to do something about it. The piling up of verbs emphasizes his determination to act: " 'I have seen . . . and have heard . . . I know . . . I have come down . . . I will send you' " (3:7-10).

Canaan is described here for the first time as a land "flowing with milk and honey" (v. 8). Actually it was not as fertile as many of the lands surrounding it. To the Israelites entering it from the desert, however, it seemed to be a paradise.

Verse 8 mentions six of the peoples living in the land before the Israelites arrived. The reason for mentioning all six was probably to reassure Israel that it was a spacious land. If it could hold six nations all at once, it could surely accommodate the tribes of Israel.

The first people mentioned are the *Canaanites.* They occupied the Mediterranean coastland and the valleys. Their name was derived from the purple dye which they produced and which was used in the making of expensive cloth. Next in order are the *Hittites.* These were of Indo-European origin. They established a great empire centering in what is now Turkey. Their empire flourished until around 1200 B.C. Some Hittites are known by name in the Old Testament, such as Ephron (Gen. 23:10) and Uriah (2 Sam. 11:3). The *Amorites* had migrated from Syria and Mesopotamia, where they were known as "Amurru." They occupied the hill country of Canaan (Num. 13:29). The term *Perrizites* seems to designate a class of peasants living in unwalled villages. The *Hivites* are usually identified with the ancient Horites, or Hurrians. They were found at various places in Canaan, including Shechem

(Gen. 34:2), Gibeon (Josh. 9:7), and Mount Lebanon (Judg. 3:3). The last people mentioned are the *Jebusites*. They were the inhabitants of Jerusalem before David captured it (2 Sam. 5:6-8).

The climax to Moses' experience at the burning bush comes in verse 10. The vision of God is followed by the command to go. He hears God saying to him, " 'Come, I will send you to Pharaoh that you may bring forth my people, the sons of Israel, out of Egypt.' "

Verse 11 contains the first of five objections that Moses raised against accepting the divine commission. The objections cover a wide range. Some are based on genuine modesty and a sense of inadequacy. Others are based on fear, especially the fear of rejection from the Israelites and resistance from Pharaoh. Others are based on nothing more than Moses' own stubborn self-will.

In dealing with his reluctant servant, God remained patient but resolute. Moses' personality was respected. He was not treated like a robot who had no choice but to obey. His objections were treated with the utmost seriousness. At the same time, he was not allowed to wiggle out of his responsibility. God would not allow him to upset his redemptive plan for Israel. Moses may have wanted to drag his feet. He even may have proposed compromises in the divine plan. But in the end he spoke for God in spite of himself.

Moses' first objection is a reflection of his modesty. He asked, " 'Who am I that I should go to Pharaoh, and bring the sons of Israel out of Egypt?' " (3:11). He did not feel that he was prepared either by personal endowment or by previous experience to undertake such a tremendous task. Moses felt that he was being called to serve God not at the point of his strength but at the point of his weakness. He was to learn, as Paul learned later, that God's strength is made perfect in our weakness (see 2 Cor. 12:7-10).

God responded to Moses' first objection by offering him a sign (v. 12). Signs are given in the Old Testament to confirm the truth of what has been spoken by God or his prophet (1 Sam. 10:7,9; 2 Kings 20:8-9; Isa. 7:11,14). Their purpose is to make believers out of skeptics.

The exact nature of the sign promised to Moses is not clear. Some interpreters think it refers to the burning bush. Others believe that the sign is the promise of the abiding presence of God with his servant. As the text now stands, however, the sign is that Israel will one day be freed from Egypt and will serve God on this same mountain. Only when Moses' efforts were crowned with success would he know for a certainty that God had sent him. Meanwhile he was to go ahead. Such a call as this demands utmost faith.

4. God Reveals His Name *(3:13-22)*

The second objection Moses raised was that he did not know the name of the God who was sending him to Egypt. If the Israelites asked him for his name, what would he tell them?

Among the ancient Hebrews a person's name stood for the person himself—his character, his attributes, his very being. Therefore, when Moses asked to know God's name, he was in fact asking God to make known his essential character.

God's reply to Moses is anything but clear. Bible interpreters are not at all sure what it means. God said to Moses, " 'I AM WHO I AM.' " He also commanded Moses to say to the Israelites, " 'I AM has sent me to you.' " Verse 15 gives his name as "The LORD," and identifies him as "the God of your fathers, the God of Abraham, the God of Isaac, and the God of Jacob."

Various interpretations have been suggested for the clause "I AM WHO I AM." Some readers see it as deliberately vague. They think God does not wish to reveal his name. "I AM WHO I AM" is therefore taken to mean, "It's no business of yours who I am." Those who take this position say that if men knew God's name, they would be tempted to use it to manipulate him. Furthermore, the nature of God cannot be fully expressed in a name. It must forever remain a mystery.

Other interpreters point out that the clause might also be translated, "I will be what I will be." Here the stress is upon the adequacy of God to meet any need that may arise in the future. Moses and Israel were to go forward in the confidence that his help would be made available as they needed it.

Albright has proposed an interpretation that has gained wide support.[1] By changing the verbs from the active to the causative, and from the first person to the third, he renders the clause, "He causes to be what comes into existence." He interprets the divine name Yahweh, which we shall discuss below, as an abbreviated form of this clause, and interprets it, "He causes to be." He views this as a fitting name for Israel's God. It stresses his role as Creator of the universe.

In any event, Moses heard the awesome name of God for the first time (see Ex. 6:2-3). In the Hebrew text, which originally consisted only of consonants, the name by which God revealed himself to Moses contained the four letters YHWH. No one knows how or even whether to translate it. The name itself is regarded by Jews as so holy that even today no Orthodox Jew will take it upon his lips. When Jewish readers encounter it in their scrolls, they substitute for it the word *Adonai*, meaning "Lord."

When the Old Testament was translated into Greek, YHWH was rendered *Kurios,* also meaning "Lord." Many modern versions, including King James and the Revised Standard, translate YHWH with small capital letters, "the LORD," to distinguish it from *Adonai.* Some translations combine the consonants of YHWH with the vowels of *Adonai.* The resulting word is "Jehovah," which is not a true Hebrew word but rather a hybrid word. It first appeared in writing about the sixteenth century after Christ.

Evidence seems to indicate that the original form of YHWH was "Yahweh." *The Jerusalem Bible* is one of the few translations to use Yahweh wherever YHWH occurs. To most readers of the Bible, however, Yahweh is a foreign sounding name with little meaning. The word "LORD," although not a translation of YHWH, but rather a substitution for it, still conveys the idea of majesty and sovereignty. It therefore remains the most acceptable translation. Whatever its origin may be, YHWH is used in the Old Testament to describe one who is always present to save, one who is adequate for every situation. With such a God by his side, Moses would be enabled to do the impossible.

Following the revelation of the divine name, Moses was commanded to return to Egypt. There he was to gather the elders of Israel. These were the older, leading men of the community. He was to tell them of God's plan to redeem them from bondage. Then they were to go with him to request permission from Pharaoh to leave. The reason they were to give for their request was that they might go a three days' journey into the wilderness to sacrifice to their God.

Moses was warned in advance that Pharaoh would deny their request. He would be unwilling to lose valuable slaves. Only the chastening hand of God would change his mind. When God smote Egypt with his wonders, then the Israelites would be released. Before they left, their long years of slavery were to be repaid by the Egyptians with gifts of gold, silver, and clothing. The reference to the spoiling of the Egyptians shows how completely the tables were turned. The Egyptians would be glad to pay the Israelites for the work they had compelled them to do and as an inducement to them to leave Egypt.

5. Further Excuses from Moses *(4:1-17)*

The more Moses learned about his mission the more resistant he became. His first two objections had been rather mild. They reflected his sense of modesty and his uncertainty about the name of God. His last three objections, however, were more serious. Moses did everything possible to avoid returning to Egypt. In the end, however, he was compelled to return in spite of himself. It should be said in his defense that once he had become convinced that this was God's will for him, he never turned back.

Moses' third objection was that the Israelites would not believe that the Lord had sent him. To meet this objection the Lord offered him three signs to perform before them. It should be remembered that signs were miracles performed by a prophet to prove to his listeners that his words were true. When Jesus was asked to confirm his word with such a sign, he refused to do so (Mark 8:11-12). A need for a sign is an indication of weak faith.

The three signs all had to do with the changing of one substance into another. A wooden staff was changed into a serpent. Healthy skin was made leprous. And water from the Nile was turned into blood. Most of the miracles in the Bible begin with the elements already present in the situation. When Jesus fed the hungry crowds, for example, he multiplied the loaves and fish that a lad had brought with him. Of Moses, God inquired, " 'What is that in your hand?' " God can take our meager resources and turn them into major assets.

The three signs had been given to Moses, and yet he had doubts. And so he entered his fourth protest. Knowing that his meetings with Pharaoh would demand that he speak, he argued that he was not eloquent. Literally the Hebrew reads, "I am not a man of words." Some have suggested that Moses was a stammerer, but the text gives no indication of this. It simply suggests that he felt inadequate as an orator. In a similar situation the prophet Jeremiah exclaimed, " 'Ah, Lord, God! Behold, I do not know how to speak, for I am only a youth' " (Jer. 1:6).

Moses heard God's response, and he was left without excuse. He was reminded that it is the Lord who has made man's mouth. It is he who assigns to men their abilities as well as their disabilities. What matters to him is not always a person's ability but his availability. The Creator of the universe can cause even the dumb to speak. Again the imperative is sounded. Moses was to go; and as he went, he was to believe that the one who made his mouth would go with him and make possible his speaking what was required.

Moses had run out of excuses. And he was still determined not to go. Now comes his fifth objection. He simply told God to get someone else to do the job. Let him send anyone he desired, that is, anyone except Moses. At this objection God finally lost his patience. Moses' flat refusal to go had made God angry.

To meet Moses' final objection, God made an adjustment in his plans. Aaron, the brother of Moses, is introduced here. He had apparently stayed in Egypt when Moses fled. God agreed that Aaron would share Moses' burden of responsibility. He would act as Moses' spokesman. The relationship between the two is compared to that between a prophet and God. Just as a prophet is the messenger of God, so Aaron would be the messenger of Moses, and Moses would be to him as God. Verse 17 picks up the theme of the rod in the hand of Moses. The rod was a reminder to Moses that God would perform all that he had promised.

6. Moses' Departure from Midian *(4:18-31)*

After the burning bush experience Moses returned to his father-in-law. He asked leave of him to return to Egypt. He did not explain why he wished to return. He simply told Jethro that he wished to visit his kinsmen to see whether they were still alive. It is a sign of the maturity of Moses that he reported to his father-in-law rather than simply leaving the country.

God commanded Moses to return to Egypt and do the miracles that he had placed in his power (v. 21). He warned him, however, that Pharaoh's heart would be hardened and that he would refuse to let the people go. Israel is called God's firstborn son in verse 22. This serves to sharpen the warning in verse 23. If Pharaoh did not release God's son, then God would slay Pharaoh's firstborn son. This is in anticipation of the tenth plague.

One of the most obscure passages in the book of Exodus is 4:24-26. On the way back to Egypt, God met Moses and sought to slay him.

Some interpreters believe that this statement is an ancient way of explaining a sudden illness that befell Moses. Since God was regarded as directly responsible for everything that happened in a person's life, Moses' illness is interpreted as God's attack on Moses. Zipporah, his wife, acted quickly and saved his life. She did three things. First, she took a flint knife and circumcised her son. Second, she touched someone's "feet" with the foreskin. "Feet" is probably a euphemism for the genital organs. The Hebrew simply reads "his feet" without specifying whether it refers to Moses or to the child. Presumably it refers to Moses. The third action of Zipporah was to say to the one whom she had touched, " 'You are a bridegroom of blood to me!' " Whatever the reason for Zipporah's strange actions, they achieved their purpose. God let Moses live.

The story dramatizes the demand for circumcision. A question it leaves unanswered is whether Moses himself had been circumcised. Certainly he had omitted to circumcise his son. That omission almost cost him his life. Some interpreters say that Moses himself had never been circumcised. But when Zipporah circumcised her son and rubbed the bloody foreskin on Moses' "feet," the son's circumcision served for both of them. No one has yet found a satisfactory explanation for Zipporah's words, " 'You are a bridegroom of blood to me!' "

After this strange experience, Moses went forward to meet Aaron. He shared with him all that God had revealed to him. The two brothers then gathered together all the elders of Israel. Aaron spoke all the words of the Lord to them and performed the signs that had been given to Moses. The result of this initial contact was favorable. The people believed, and when they heard that God had visited them in their affliction, they bowed their heads and worshiped. It was a happy beginning.

7. Lessons for Life from the Scriptures

God is still relieving the oppressed in the world today. This may not be apparent always; nevertheless, it is true. In fact, we can be sure that if God is present anywhere in the world today, it is beside the poor and the oppressed. These were the people that Jesus sought to help during his earthly ministry. And he confirmed what the Old Testament prophets had taught. It is that God is the friend of the friendless, the redeeming God, the God who acts (see Jas. 5:1-4).

God works through the instrumentality of men and women whom he calls into his service. This has always been so. The delivery of the Israelites out of Egypt had to be delayed until Moses was ready to answer God's call. We are God's hands and feet to minister to a needy world. And so the question is not, Why is God not doing more to relieve suffering? but, Why are we not doing more? God acts through men and women.

And still he is not without his army of servants today. All around the world, often in out-of-the-way places, dedicated Christians are ministering to others in his name. Some of these persons are ordained, but most are not. And this makes no difference to him. His will is that every born-again believer answer his call to serve a needy world.

It is still possible for us to resist the call of God for our lives. God had a mighty mission for Moses, but Moses preferred to remain a simple shepherd. He was willing to settle for easy success rather than risk great failure. There are many like Moses in the world today. God has a magnificent plan for their lives, but they are afraid to trust their future into his hands. And because of their fear and distrust they miss their highest destiny. God meant for them to fly, but they prefer to grovel in the dust.

When one entrusts his life to God, God more than makes up for all his servant's inadequacies and deficiencies. Moses is a prime example of the truth of this statement. But there are many, many more. One of J.B. Tidwell's former students reports his saying frequently, " 'One man plus God equals enough.' " Paul said, "I can do all things in him who strengthens me" (Phil. 4:13). What matters most to God is not always our ability but our availability.

----

[1]William F. Albright, *Yahweh and the Gods of Canaan* (Garden City: Doubleday and Company, Inc., 1968), pp. 168-172.

Personal Learning Activities

1. Dr. Kelley identifies five elements of biblical call narratives. From the list below select those five elements:
   ____ (1) An encounter with God.
   ____ (2) A promise of success.
   ____ (3) God's spoken command.
   ____ (4) Two kinds of responses.
   ____ (5) Forewarning of rejection.
   ____ (6) Promised exemption from trouble.
   ____ (7) Assurance of God's presence.
2. Moses' commission included three plain facts. From the list below identify those facts as stated in the text:
   ____ (1) God's resolution to rescue Israel from bondage;
   ____ (2) God's purpose to set Israel in a favored position;
   ____ (3) God's choice of Moses as deliverer;
   ____ (4) Pharaoh's opposition to God's plan;
   ____ (5) Moses' reluctance to undertake the task.
3. In God's commissioning of Moses to deliver Israel from Egypt, God answered Moses' second of five objections by declaring his (God's) name to be YHWH: True ____ False ____
4. The following meanings for God's covenant name with Israel were discussed in the textbook (select correct responses):
   ____ (1) The name is deliberately vague—"It's no business of yours."
   ____ (2) The name stresses God's adequacy for the future—"I will be what I will be."
   ____ (3) The name stresses God's role as Creator of the universe—"He causes to be."
   ____ (4) The name compasses God's deathless existence—"I am that I am."
5. Enumerate in their proper order Moses' objections to God's call to service:
   ____ (1) The Israelites would not believe the Lord had sent him.
   ____ (2) Moses did not know the Lord's name.
   ____ (3) Moses felt inadequate for the task.
   ____ (4) Moses asked God to get someone else.
   ____ (5) Moses protested he could not speak.
6. Which, if any, of the excuses Moses offered God for not serving have you used? Which, if any, are you using right now?

Answers:
1. (1),(3),(4),(5),(7); 2. (1), (2), (3); 3. True; 4. (1), (2), (3); 5. 3,2,1,5,4; 5. Your answer.

God Reveals His Power

Exodus 5:1 to 10:29

In the previous study of God's call and man's response we saw how Moses escaped to Midian only to hear God's call to return to Egypt. Moses was not allowed to retire from the world and its problems even though he may have wanted to do so. Neither can we retreat from the world and its problems in our day.

A man may escape from his normal environment, but he cannot escape from himself or from God. And it is only as one is confronted by God that he is compelled to ask, "Who am I?" (see 3:11). A person can never discover his true identity except in relationship to God. Moses came face to face with God and was impelled to re-examine his own nature and destiny in the light of that awesome experience. He would never have found himself if God had not found him first.

The second part of Moses' reaction is revealed in the question in 3:13. The essence of this question is, "Who is God?" Moses wanted to know whether the God who had appeared to him in the burning bush was worthy of the belief, trust, and commitment of Israel.

Moses' two questions reveal the nature of his inward struggle. Basically, therefore, his response to God boils down to two questions of identification: "Who am I?" and "Who is God?" Who Moses was had to be linked with who God is. In like manner Israel's character and destiny were inseparably linked to her concept of God. What people believe about God *does* make a difference in personal development.

1. The Egyptian Concept of Kingship

Before studying the account of the plagues, let us briefly examine the

ancient Egyptian concept of kingship. This will help us to understand
the true nature of the struggle between God and Pharaoh.

From the beginning of the Old Kingdom in Egypt (about 2800 B.C.)
through the time of the Exodus, the Egyptian concept of kingship remained unchanged. Dynasties might change and capitals move from
city to city, but the Egyptians persisted in their belief that their
pharaohs were divine.[1]

The pharaohs did everything possible to strengthen belief in their
divinity. They built the great pyramids, for example, with this purpose
in mind. These were actually royal tombs made to resemble mountains.
They were designed to resist decay to the maximum. The cost of their
construction was enormous, both in men and materials. The pyramid
tombs were symbolic in two respects. First, their enduring shape and
construction asserted a belief in the immortality of the king who was
buried within. Second, the Egyptians did not count the cost, since they
were building an eternal home for their god-king. They thought that
such a cause was worthy of their best efforts in time, materials, man-
power, and craftsmanship. In sublime arrogance these royal tombs
dominated early Egyptian history and sent their shadows down across
the ages.

Egyptian mythology is filled with stories which place the pharaohs
among the gods. It is difficult for us to understand how rational people
could actually accept such a belief. But all evidence points to the fact
that the Egyptians did believe their kings were gods, and their kings
believed it about themselves.

When this belief in the divinity of pharaoh was applied to life, it led
to devastating results, especially where the Hebrews were concerned. It
meant, for example, that the Pharaoh's word with the Hebrews was
abolute law. He held the power of life and death over his subjects. And
since slavery was considered to be vital to his country's economy, he
did not hesitate to enslave foreign groups such as the Hebrews. Furthermore, since he occupied the place of god, the practice of any other
religion by the inhabitants to Egypt would be considered as idolatry
and blasphemy. This helps to explain the Hebrew's request that they be
allowed to leave Egypt in order to sacrifice to the Lord their God in the
wilderness. It also helps us to understand why the Pharaoh turned
down their request.

2. God's Claim on Israel

The key to understanding God's claim on Israel is given in 4:22-23:
" 'You shall say to Pharaoh, "Thus says the Lord, Israel is my first-

born son, and I say to you, 'Let my son go that he may serve me'; if you refuse to let him go, behold, I will slay your first-born son.'' ' ''

The drama in this setting is compelling. On one side stood the Pharaoh, who asserted his right to enslave the Hebrews and to exploit them to the fullest. On the other side stood God, claiming the Hebrews as his sons and proclaiming his intention to set them free. The battle lines thus were drawn between the god-king of Egypt and the mighty God of Israel.

There was never any doubt about the final outcome. Nothing in human history could ultimately defeat the divine purpose. In spite of his ancient claim to divinity, the Pharaoh was reduced to mortal stature. Exodus 10:1-2 puts the matter in its proper perspective, "Then the Lord said to Moses, 'Go in to Pharaoh; for I have hardened his heart and the heart of his servants, that I may show these signs of mine among them, and that you may tell in the hearing of your son and of your son's son how I made sport of the Egyptians and what signs I have done among them; that they may know that I am the Lord.' ''

3. The Hardening of Pharaoh's Heart
When the Lord called Moses, he said to him, " 'When you go back to Egypt, see that you do before Pharaoh all the miracles which I have put in your power; but I will harden his heart, so that he will not let the people go' '' (4:21). In several later passages we are told that the Lord did harden the Pharaoh's heart, with the result that he refused to listen to Moses and Aaron or to let the children of Israel go (see 7:3-4; 9:12; 10:20).

Alongside these references to God's hardening the heart of the Pharaoh are others which place the responsibility for this hardening upon Pharaoh himself. "When Pharaoh saw that there was a respite, he hardened his heart, and would not listen to them; as the Lord had said" (8:15; see also 8:32; 9:34).

The author of Exodus makes no attempt to resolve this paradox of human freedom and divine sovereignty. Repeatedly he stated that the Lord hardened Pharaoh's heart, while affirming that Pharaoh hardened his own heart. Pharaoh was a free moral agent pursuing his own course of action and fully responsible for his own misdeeds, but from the author's viewpoint the Lord never surrendered his control of the situation. Pharaoh was given plenty of rope, but the end of the rope was always held firmly in the Lord's hands. Pharaoh could not run beyond the bounds of God's sovereign control.

Three different Hebrew verbs are employed by the author of Exodus to describe the hardening of Pharaoh's heart. The one used most frequently means "to hold fast, be strong, make obstinate." It suggests a stubborn, unyielding disposition. The second verb means "to be heavy or dull." It describes moral and spiritual insensitivity. The third, which appears only once (7:3), means "to stiffen or make severe." It suggests a harsh and stubborn resistance to the will of God. Through the combined use of these verbs the author portrayed Pharaoh as being unyielding, insensitive, and stubborn.

The central purpose in the hardening of Pharaoh's heart is represented as being didactic. That is, God wanted to teach future generations in Israel how he made sport of the Egyptians by performing his signs among them and how he brought his people out of bondage (10:1-2; see also Deut. 6:20-25). Paul understood this didactic purpose when he wrote later concerning Pharaoh, "The scripture says to Pharaoh, 'I have raised you up for the very purpose of showing my power in you, so that my name may be proclaimed in all the earth' " (Rom. 9:17).

One of the most significant statements made in the context of Pharaoh's hardening of his own heart is that of the magicians as recorded in 8:19. After they had tried to imitate Aaron and to bring forth gnats by their secret arts, but without success, they exclaimed to Pharaoh, " 'This is the finger of God.' "

The finger of God refers in a unique way to the revelation of God's power. This expression occurs only four times in the Scriptures. We read in Exodus 8:19 that the signs and wonders that resulted in the liberation of God's people from Egypt were wrought by the finger of God. Later at Sinai the law was inscribed on tables of stone by the finger of God (Ex. 31:18). In Psalm 8:3 we are told that the heavens are the work of God's fingers. Finally, in Luke 11:20 we learn that Jesus spoke of casting out demons by the finger of God. When these four references are seen together, they portray the manifestation of God's power in creation, in the Exodus, in the giving of the Law at Sinai, and in the incarnation. Truly, "Great is the Lord and greatly to be praised!" (Ps. 48:1).

4. A Discouraging Beginning (5:1 to 6:1)

After Moses and Aaron had met with the elders of Israel (4:29-31), they went to Pharaoh. They presented themselves proudly before the king and addressed him as messengers of the Lord, the God of Israel. Their claim to authority was reinforced by their opening words, "Thus says the Lord," a formula usually employed in the Old Testament to introduce a prophet's speech. It is used frequently throughout the story of Moses and Aaron's encounters with the Pharaoh (7:17; 8:1; 9:1,13; 10:3). In refusing to let the children of Israel go, Pharaoh was not resisting Moses and Aaron alone but even the Lord God himself.

The initial meeting with Pharaoh ended in complete failure. The divine plan was temporarily sidetracked, and the situation of the Hebrew slaves worsened. Pharaoh scoffed at the request that they be permitted to go a three days' journey into the wilderness to hold a feast to the Lord their God. He probably suspected that this was but a ploy on their part to escape from bondage and that they did not intend to return to Egypt.

Pharaoh arrogantly denied that he knew a god named the Lord (5:2). The theme of his not knowing the Lord is played up throughout the account of the plagues. The writer takes great delight in showing how through the plagues Pharaoh was introduced to the Lord. Before they were over, both he and all his people knew very well who the Lord was (see 7:5,17; 8:10; 9:29). The plagues were sent not so much to soften Pharaoh's heart as to glorify God's power and authority. When a person refuses to know the Lord in obedience, he will know him in judgment.

When Moses requested that the people of Israel be permitted to go into the wilderness to serve their God (5:1), Pharaoh's retort was, " 'Go now, and work; for no straw shall be given you, yet you shall deliver the same number of bricks' " (5:18). The same Hebrew verb is used in these two verses to mean both "to serve" and "to work." Pharaoh was throwing Moses' words back in his face. He was saying, in effect, "If the Israelites want to serve someone, I'll see to it that they have ample opportunity to serve me!"

Pharaoh gave orders for the work load of the Hebrews to be increased. The slave laborers not only had to produce the same number of bricks, but had to scout around and find straw that was used to hold the mud bricks together. Sun-dried mud bricks made with straw as a binder have been used as building materials in Egypt from prehistoric times to the present.

Under these conditions the people found the quotas assigned to them impossible. Verse 10 refers to taskmasters and foremen. The former apparently were Egyptians and the latter Hebrews. The Hebrew foremen were responsible to their Egyptian bosses to see that the people delivered their daily quota of bricks. When the people failed to do this, the Hebrew foremen were beaten (5:14). Their protest to Pharaoh only brought this reply, " 'You are idle, you are idle; therefore you say, "Let us go and sacrifice to the Lord" ' " (5:17). Pharaoh was saying, in effect: "Your people don't have enough work to do. That is why they are demanding a vacation."

The foremen then turned upon Moses and Aaron and blamed them for all their troubles (5:20-21). This was exactly the effect that Pharaoh had hoped for. The agitators were discredited. Instead of carrying out their promise to liberate the people, Moses and Aaron had involved them in worse trouble.

Even Moses was discouraged at the disastrous turn of events. It was the first setback that he had encountered, and it took him unawares. However, it must be said to his credit that he met it with prayer. He laid his troubles squarely before the Lord. He asked, " 'O Lord . . . why didst thou ever send me?' " (5:22). Not only had he been rejected by his own brethren, but it seemed as though God also had abandoned him. His anguished cry might be compared to that of Jesus on the cross, " 'My God, my God, why hast thou forsaken me?' " (Mark 15:34). But at that moment God gave his reassuring reply, " 'Now you shall see what I will do to Pharaoh' " (6:1). The final outcome of the situation would demonstrate that God was able to do more than Moses even dared believe.

5. A Reaffirmation of Moses' Call *(6:2 to 7:7)*
The call account in 6:2 to 7:7 is roughly parallel to that found in 3:1 to 4:31. God's review of Moses' call at this point in the story was meant to bolster Moses' failing courage. At this critical moment, when Moses was despondent over his initial setback, God gave him a fresh word of revelation.

As in the earlier account (3:13-15) God disclosed to Moses his covenant name—*Yahweh,* translated "Lord." Exodus 6:3 states that although the patriarchs worshiped the same God as Moses, they did not know him by the name "Lord." This verse implies that there are stages or periods in God's revelation to Israel. In the beginning God had simply been called "God" (Hebrew: *Elohim*). Later he revealed himself to Abraham by a new name—*El Shaddai*, translated "God Almighty" (Gen. 17:1). The exact meaning of this name is uncertain, although it probably means "Mountain God." The climactic step in God's revelation of his name came when he disclosed himself to Moses as *Yahweh*, "Lord." This new name implied a new relationship between God and Israel. *Yahweh* (Lord) is the covenant name of God, affirming the covenant that he established with Israel.

Perhaps the most important feature in this recounting of the call of

Moses is the identification in 6:6 of God as Redeemer. Here God plainly stated, " ' "I will redeem you with an outstretched arm and with great acts of judgment." ' " The only earlier use of the verb "to redeem" is in Genesis 48:16, in the blessing of Jacob. This is therefore one of the golden texts of the Bible, for it introduces us to one of the most significant concepts in biblical theology.

From the verb "to redeem" comes the noun *go'el,* translated "redeemer." The term is technical and grew out of ancient tribal and family law. A *go'el* in ancient Israel was a man's near kinsman who assumed certain responsibilities on his behalf. For example, when someone was forced by poverty to sell himself into slavery, his *go'el* was obligated to purchase his freedom (Lev. 25:47-54). Or if poverty forced an Israelite to sell his ancestral lands, then his *go'el* must redeem these also (Lev. 25:25). A particular duty of the *go'el* was to marry the childless widow of his deceased brother in order to beget children to preserve his brother's name (Gen. 38:7-8; Deut. 25:5-10; Ruth 2:20; 3:12; 4:1-12). This type of marriage is technically known as a levirate marriage.

In addition to these responsibilities, the *go'el* was under obligation to avenge the blood of any murdered kinsman (Num. 35:16-21). This type of blood vengeance rested on the two-fold principle of the sacredness of blood (Lev. 17:14) and the solidarity of the tribe or family.

For God to say that he would redeem Israel meant two things. First, it meant that the covenant bonds that linked Israel to God and God to Israel were as intimate and as strong as family ties. Second, it meant that no sacrifice was too demanding and no price too great for God to pay for the redemption of his people. And this should remind us that Israel's *go'el* is also our Redeemer-Kinsman.

6. Signs and Wonders *(7:8 to 10:29)*

This section describes a series of nine plagues which came upon the Egyptians. The tenth and climactic plague resulted in the death of the Egyptian firstborn. The telling of this plague is delayed until Exodus 12, where it is connected with the initial celebration of the Feast of the Passover.

The Old Testament frequently refers to the plagues as "signs and wonders" (Deut. 4:34; 6:22; 26:8; Pss. 78:43; 105:27). Signs and wonders include all natural phenomena or historical events that appear awe inspiring, mysterious, surprising, or astonishing. In the Old Testament, signs and wonders never stand alone, but are closely linked with the word of God. God never acts merely to startle and amaze men. Signs and wonders were intended to say something to men. The plagues therefore were meant to convince Pharaoh that God indeed had sent Moses to liberate the Israelites. In addition to this, they reminded the Israelites that their liberation had come about not because of any shrewdness or strength on their part, but because of the invincible power of their God.

The story of the plagues is told in a highly dramatic fashion. The suspense mounts as each succeeding plague becomes more destructive than the previous one. Those surrounding the Pharaoh are gradually forced to acknowledge the power of Moses' God. Even the court magicians see in the plagues the finger of God (8:19). All are convinced except Pharaoh himself. It takes the tenth and final plague to bring him to his knees at last.

The story of Pharaoh's gradual softening toward Moses' demands is told with great skill. He was unmoved by the transforming of Aaron's rod into a serpent (7:8-13). Even the first two plagues made little impression on him. In fact, his magicians were able to reproduce the first two plagues (7:22; 8:7). After the third plague, however, Pharaoh was willing to let the Hebrews sacrifice to their God, provided they stayed in the land of Egypt (8:25). When Moses refused to compromise on this point, Pharaoh offered to let the Israelites go a short distance outside the land and sacrifice to their God (8:28). After the seventh plague Pharaoh confessed that he had sinned and offered to let the Hebrews go, only to harden his heart soon afterwards (9:27-28,34). He then tried to negotiate another compromise with Moses. He offered to let the men go if they would leave their wives and children behind in Egypt (10:8-11). Once again Moses would not agree to such a compromise. After the ninth plague Pharaoh offered to let all the Israelites go, but without their flocks and herds (10:24). Moses' bold reply to this compromise was, " 'Our cattle also must go with us; not a hoof shall be left behind' " (10:26). It was only after the plague of death on all the firstborn among the Egyptians that Pharaoh finally surrendered to Moses' demands.

The four compromises proposed by Pharaoh at different stages during these negotiations are instructive. They may be stated as follows: (1) "Stay in Egypt"; (2) "Don't go very far away"; (3) "Leave your wives and children behind"; and (4) "Leave your flocks and herds behind." The same four compromises are proposed to us in our Christian pilgrimage. We are urged to remain in "Egypt," the land of servitude and bondage to sin. If we choose to leave this land, we are urged not to go very far away, to be borderline Christians. Again, we are tempted to neglect the spiritual care and nurture of our families, especially our children. Finally, we are urged not to commit our "flocks and herds" to the Lord, that is, to compromise in the area of the stewardship of possessions. In the face of these temptations we should be prepared to say with Moses, " 'We will go with our young and our old; we will go with our sons and daughters and with our flocks and herds, for we must hold a feast to the Lord' " (10:9).

Cassuto[2] has pointed out that the first nine plagues fall into three cycles of three plagues each. In each cycle the first and second plagues come after Pharaoh has been warned, whereas the third plague in each cycle comes without warning. Also before the first plague in each cycle Moses meets Pharaoh outdoors, whereas before the second plague in each cycle he meets him indoors, in the palace. We may illustrate this in the following table:

1st Cycle	2nd Cycle	3rd Cycle	Prelude
1. Blood	4. Flies	7. Hail	Warning given: Moses meets Pharaoh outdoors
2. Frogs	5. Cattle plague	8. Locusts	Warning given: Moses meets Pharaoh indoors
3. Gnats	6. Boils	9. Darkness	No warning given

The plagues are listed not only here but also in Psalms 78:43-51 and 105:28-36. However, the two lists in the Psalms do not agree at every point with the list given in Exodus. Various explanations have been given for the differences, but none is entirely satisfactory. The plague material appears in the New Testament only in chapters 8, 16 of Revelation, and then only in an altered form. Revelation 16 pictures seven bowls of judgment in terms of boils, water turned to blood, death of fish, fierce heat, darkness, foul spirits like frogs, and lightning, thunder, and earthquake. The repetition of the phrase "they did not repent and give him glory" (Rev. 16:9,11) recalls the stubborn resistance of Pharaoh.

A new element is introduced into the story of the ten plagues beginning with the fourth one. It is that a distinction is made between the Israelites and the Egyptians 8:22; 9:4,26; 10:22-23; 11:6-7). This theme is repeated often until it comes to a climax in the final separation of Israel from Egypt by the blood on the doorpost, which protects from the death angel.

If often has been noted that the plagues involved many natural phenomena that were common to Egypt. These included such things as frogs, gnats, flies, boils, hail, and locusts. The Egyptian magicians were even able to match some of the feats of Aaron, such as the changing of the rod into a serpent (7:10-11), the turning of water into blood (7:20,22), and the bringing up of frogs over the land (8:6-7). The thick darkness (10:22) may have resulted from a strong wind blowing in from the desert. The modern name for such a wind is *khamsin* (Arabic for "fifty," since it occurs during the fifty days of spring). A *khamsin* sprang up suddenly, brought intense heat and thick clouds of dust, and caused darkness wherever it went. This writer witnessed a *khamsin* in Jerusalem on the Thursday evening before Easter in 1973. A strong east wind brought intense heat and so much dust that the full moon was blotted out, and the sun did not appear all day on Good Friday. It was an awesome experience.

However, while many of the plagues involved natural phenomena, they are presented as mighty acts of God. When we argue about whether the plagues were natural or supernatural, we are using categories that were completely foreign to the people of the ancient time. They never thought of any phenomenon or event as being natural, that is, as caused by laws that operated automatically and apart from God's immediate supervision. The Hebrews had no word in their language that meant "nature." They saw the hand of God in all events, even those that a scientifically oriented person might have regarded as caused by natural laws. The ancient Hebrews would have agreed with Chesterton's insightful remark, "The sun does not rise by natural law, but because God says 'Get up and do it again.' "[3]

The story of the plagues is not simply an objective recounting of events but a record of events as seen through the eyes of faith. Ancient Hebrews saw the hand of God in these events for four reasons. The first was that they came in rapid succession. The second was their intensity and severity. The third was that they were foretold by Moses. And the fourth was that they occurred at a precise moment in history and resulted in the liberation of the Israelites. People of faith affirm with the Bible that these signs and wonders were the mighty acts of God.

We might conclude this study of the plagues by recalling the words of Paul in Romans 9:17, "Scripture says to Pharaoh, 'I have raised you up for this very purpose, to exhibit my power in my dealings with you, and to spread my fame over all the world' " (NEB).[4] Note that we have entitled this chapter in our study, "God Reveals His Power."

7. Lessons for Life from the Scriptures

One never gets too old to serve the Lord. According to 7:7, Moses was eighty years old when he returned to Egypt to free the Israelites. In his seeking to be excused from this difficult mission, Moses never mentioned his age as a negative force. Too often in our day older persons have simply given up. They see a world that needs to be changed, but they are willing to leave this task to the younger generation. And all too often the younger generation lacks the wisdom and maturity to get the job done. It takes all of us working together to do the Lord's work.

Great leaders are God's gift to mankind. The significance of Moses and the role he played in the Exodus experience is impossible to overemphasize. Numbers 12:3 testifies to his greatness, "The man Moses was very meek, more than all men that were on the face of the earth." Moses was always able to keep himself in the background so that the movement he started was stamped with the divine name and not his own. Fleming James has written, "Alone among the great historic religions of mankind that of Moses is not called after its founder."[5] The New Testament bears further witness to Moses' greatness in these words, "He considered abuse suffered for the Christ greater wealth than the treasures of Egypt, for he looked to the reward" (Heb. 11:26).

In a famous Egyptian story an Egyptian nobleman named Sinuhe had to flee his country for political reasons. He joined a desert tribe of nomads and eventually rose to be their chief. When he had grown old, however, he became homesick. Leaving a son to rule in his stead, he bade farewell to the harsh life of the desert and returned to spend his last days in his native Egypt.[6]

Moses chose to do the exact opposite. He chose to cast his lot with a nondescript group of Hebrew slaves and to leave Pharaoh's court for the uncertain life of the desert. Once he had made his decision, he carried it out. He was characterized as a man of humility, patience, and perseverance.

Moses' spirit of humility and his willingness to sacrifice personal ambition in the pursuit of a ministry to others remind us of Christ. Paul wrote concerning him: "Have this mind among yourselves, which you have in Christ Jesus, who, though he was in the form of God, did not count equality with God a thing to be grasped, but emptied himself, taking the form of a servant, being born in the likeness of men. And being found in human form he humbled himself and became obedient unto death, even death on a cross" (Phil. 2:5-8).

History is not governed by chance nor by the nation with the largest army. The poor, miserable people of Israel seemed no match for the strong armies of Pharaoh, but they had the mighty power of God to back them up. The Bible teaches that God is always on the side of the oppressed against their oppressors. God is the champion and defender of such defenseless members of society as the foreigner, the widow, the orphan, and the slave (see Deut. 15:12-15; 24:17-18, 21-22).

Pharaoh represents all the tyrants of history who have risen to power by crushing others. Although for a moment he seemed invincible, it was God and not he who was the sovereign ruler of history. Even though Pharaoh seemed to have immense freedom, the boundaries of that freedom were in God's hands. He could breathe out his threats against the tiny group of Israelites and fill the air with his bombast, but it was God and not he who had the final word. Pharaoh had yet to learn that history is "his-story," the story of God's mighty acts in history to fulfill his purpose for his people and for all mankind.

Dictators and tyrants do not change. They behave in exactly the same way, whether their campaigns are fought in the thirteenth century B.C. with sword and spear or in the twentieth century with jets and guided missiles. They scream the same threats and make the same boasts, whatever their language. But when the dust of battle has settled and they are forgotten, God is the ruler yet.

God is concerned about the physical needs of people as well as their spiritual needs. Of course he is concerned that men be redeemed from spiritual bondage. His Son came that the shackles of sin might be broken. But he is also concerned that men be rescued from bondage to hunger, poverty, disease, and oppression. Surely if God is present and active anywhere in the world today, it is beside the hungry, the diseased, and the oppressed. And Jesus taught that when we render service to such as these, we are actually rendering service to him (Matt. 25:34-40). The Salvation Army has long operated on the rule that if hungry and dirty men are given soup and soap, they will be better disposed to hear the gospel. The truth in this philosophy is clear. (See Jas. 2:14-17.)

We hear a lot of talk today about freedom: religious freedom, academic freedom, personal freedom, political freedom, economic freedom, freedom from want, freedom from fear, freedom from ignorance, freedom of speech. These are all noble concepts, but do we really believe they are important? Do we desire these freedoms for ourselves alone or for all men everywhere? Would we be as willing as Moses to sacrifice personal ambition in order that others might be free? The way in which we as Americans answer these questions will determine what kind of nation we become in the third century of our existence.

———
¹John A Wilson, *The Culture of Ancient Egypt* (Chicago: The University of Chicago Press, 1951), pp. 69-103.

²U. Cassuto, *A Commentary on the Book of Exodus,* trans. Israel Abrahams (Jerusalem: The Magnes Press, 1967), pp. 92-93.

³Bernhard W. Anderson, *Understanding the Old Testament,* 3rd ed. (Englewood Cliffs: Prentice-Hall, Inc., 1957). p. 43.

⁴From *The New English Bible.* © The Delegates of the Oxford University Press and the Syndics of the Cambridge University Press 1961, 1970. Reprinted by permission. All succeeding quotations from this version are indicated by specific statement or the abbreviation NEB.

⁵Fleming James, *Personalities of the Old Testament* (New York: Charles Scribner's Sons, 1951), p. 13.

⁶James B. Pritchard, ed., *Ancient Near Eastern Texts* (Princeton: Princeton University Press, 1955), pp. 18-22.

Personal Learning Activities

1. Essentially the contest in Egypt was between the god-king of Egypt and the God of Israel: True____ False____ . Why?
2. Exodus 8:25; 8:28; 10:8-11; 10:24 record the propositions Pharaoh made to Moses. From the list below identify those propositions:
   ____ (1)"Sacrifice to God within the land."
   ____ (2)"Go . . . only not very far."
   ____ (3)"Go . . . the men among you."
   ____ (4)"Send the children."
   ____ (5)"Go . . . only let your flocks and herds stay."
3. Reread the Scripture passages cited above, but as Satan's temptations to compromise the Christian's commitment. Moses rejected all the propositions. Have you?
4. Exodus 6:6 is the second Old Testament text after Genesis 48:16 (which is first) to use the word "redeem." This usage is important because (select one statement):
   ____ (1)It signifies God's intention to deliver Israel from Egypt.
   ____ (2)It introduces a significant concept of biblical theology.
5. The word "redeemer" (*go'el*) is illuminated by the following usages in Hebrew life (select the correct usages):
   ____ (1)A *go'el* was a near kinsman.
   ____ (2)A *go'el* was obliged to purchase an enslaved kinsman's freedom.
   ____ (3)A *go'el* was obliged to marry a deceased kinsman's childless widow.
   ____ (4)A *go'el* was obliged to avenge his kinsman's murder.
6. Which of the usages above relate to Jesus Christ as Redeemer? How and Why?

___

Answers:

1. *True*, your answer; 2. *(1),(2),(3),(5)*; 3. Your answer; 4. *(2)*; 5. All 4 responses; 6. Your answer.

4

God Saves His People
Exodus 11:1 to 13:16

The section before us deals primarily with the tenth plague, the celebration of the Passover, the escape of Israel from Egypt, and regulations regarding the consecration of the firstborn to the Lord.

1. The Announcement of the Last Plague *(11:1-10)*
A difference in quality marked the tenth plague from all that came before it. The first four were little more than a source of annoyance to the Egyptians. The next four were more serious, causing damage to persons and property. The ninth was a source of terror, as darkness covered the land. It was the tenth, however, that brought utter consternation and led to Pharaoh's resolve to let the people go.

The tenth plague was the climax of a great struggle between God and Pharaoh. It was a life-and-death struggle. Death would come to the firstborn of the loser. Life would be given to the firstborn of the winner (see Ex. 4:22-23). God's mighty power was never more evident in the history of ancient Israel than when he turned the tables on the Egyptians and rescued his people from a living death. By means of these mighty acts of God the Hebrews found hope in the midst of hopelessness, life in the midst of death, and freedom in the midst of slavery.

Verse 1 stresses the finality of the tenth plague. The Lord said to Moses, "'Yet one plague more I will bring upon Pharaoh and upon Egypt.'" The Hebrew word rendered here as "plague" means literally "stroke." God had yet one mighty stroke reserved for Pharaoh. In the conclusion to this verse words are heaped upon words to emphasize the urgency with which Pharaoh would send the Israelites out of his land.

The New English Bible paraphrases God's words to Moses as follows: " 'One last plague I will bring upon Pharaoh and Egypt. After that he will let you go; he will send you packing, as a man dismisses a rejected bride.' "

Verse 2 touches upon what has come to be called the despoiling of the Egyptians. At the beginning of Moses' call he had been told by the Lord, " 'I will give this people favor in the sight of the Egyptians; and when you go, you shall not go empty, but each woman shall ask of her neighbor, and of her who sojourns in her house, jewelry of silver and of gold, and clothing, and you shall put them on your sons and on your daughters; thus you shall despoil the Egyptians' " (Ex. 3:21-22). This command is repeated in 11:2, and the record of its fulfillment is found in 12:35-36. Exodus 11:3 indicates that the Egyptians were willing to share their silver and gold with the departing Israelites because of their high esteem for Moses. He was regarded as a great man in the sight of Pharaoh's officials and in the sight of the people.

The despoiling of the Egyptians has posed a problem in the minds of some readers. Was there not an element of deception in the Israelites' "borrowing" items of jewelry and clothing from their neighbors and then leaving the country without returning the borrowed items? How could the Egyptians who thus lost their valuables be held accountable for the sins of Pharaoh? These Egyptian neighbors seem to have been on fairly friendly terms with the Israelites. Such seeming misuse of trust appears to make the Israelites' action all the more questionable. The problem is complicated even further by the fact that the Lord is pictured as placing his stamp of approval on all that the Israelites did.

The modern reader therefore understandably might be offended by the seeming deception and injustice of the whole procedure. However, the Old Testament saw it in another light. Clements has summed up the matter in these words: "The spoiling of the Egyptians was to serve as a punishment for the ill-treatment of the Israelite slaves, and also as a payment for the work they had been forced to do. Thus, in the narrator's eyes, it was an act of divine justice."[1]

In other words, the Egyptians were merely being forced to do what justice demanded under the covenant law of Israel. This is most clearly set forth later in the regulations regarding slaves in Deuteronomy 15:12-15: " 'If your brother, a Hebrew man, or a Hebrew woman, is sold by you, he shall serve you six years, and in the seventh year you shall let him go free from you. And when you let him go free from you, you shall not let him go empty-handed; you shall furnish him liberally out of your flock, out of your threshing floor, and out of your wine press; as the Lord your God has blessed you, you shall give to him. You shall remember that you were a slave in the land of Egypt, and the Lord your God redeemed you; therefore I command you this today.' "

The Hebrew slaves had been in Egypt 430 years, according to Exodus 12:40-41. Consequently, they were entitled to liberation and also to the gifts that normally accompanied liberation. This was according to the law established by God. Therefore they believed they had a perfect right to ask parting gifts of the Egyptians, and that the Egyptians had a moral obligation to share their wealth with the Israelites. God in his justice would not permit the Hebrew slaves, after all their years of service, to go out of their house of bondage empty-handed.

2. The Institution of the Passover *(12:1-28)*
The narrative of Exodus slows down noticeably at this point. Minute details receive full attention. This is an indication of the importance of the subject matter.

The Bible reports that the Israelites left Egypt at midnight by the light of the full moon. It was the full moon of the spring equinox, the night of the fourteenth of Nisan, corresponding to March-April in our calendar. Since that night about thirty-two hundred years ago, the Passover has been celebrated as a memorial to the Exodus out of Egypt. This makes it the oldest continuously observed religious festival known to mankind.

Another feast, an agricultural feast, called the Feast of Unleavened Bread, began on the fifteenth of Nisan, a day later than Passover, and continued for seven days (see Ex. 12:14-20; Lev. 23:6-8; Num. 28:17-25). The Feast of Unleavened Bread probably originated to mark the end of the old season's crop of barley and the harvesting of the new season's crop. Its principal feature was the exclusion of leaven from all bread. Its link to Passover was provided by the explanation that in their haste to leave Egypt the Israelites had no time to wait until their dough was leavened (Ex.12:34). In time to come the proximity of these two feasts led to their being regarded virtually as one (see Ex. 23:15; Deut. 16:1-8).

There is special significance in the link between the Passover celebration and the Exodus event. Since the Passover was the oldest of Israel's feasts and the Exodus represented the very hour of the nation's birth, these two were inseparably bound together. Passover was the ancient Hebrews' Easter and the Fourth of July all wrapped up into one. Each time this feast was observed, they were reminded of the mighty acts of God that initiated their national history.

Exodus 12:2 states, " 'This month shall be for you the beginning of months; it shall be the first month of the year for you.' " We are told in 13:4 that the name of the month was Abib. Abib means "ears of grain," and apparently refers to the beginning of the barley harvest. When the Babylonian names of the months were taken over in the late seventh century, the month was called Nisan (see Neh. 2:1; Esther 3:7).

Moses gave detailed instructions for the observance of the Passover. The lamb for the Passover was to be selected on the tenth day of the month (Ex. 12:3) and offered on the fourteenth day of the month (Ex. 12:5). The period between the choice of the lamb and its being slaughtered gave the owner ample time to verify that it was without blemish. Exodus 12:5 suggests that a young goat was equally as acceptable as a lamb for the Passover sacrifice, although in actual practice a lamb seems always to have been used.

From the beginning Passover was a family festival; it was celebrated at home. In this respect it differed from the other major religious festivals of Israel. Exodus 12:3 specifies one lamb for each household, whereas the next verse provides for two small households to share the same lamb if necessary. At a later time Jewish authorities stipulated ten as the minimum number of persons who could gather to celebrate the Passover together.[2] Usually, however, the gatherings were much larger, and the participants ate only a small piece of the sacrificial meat. In fact, the legal minimum size of a serving was defined by later tradition as "a portion the size of an olive."[3]

The requirements for the Passover lamb are spelled out in Exodus 12:5. It had to be without blemish. This meant that it had to be sound and healthy, not sick or mutilated. It had to be a male a year old. Jews interpret this to require that the lamb be within the year of its birth and not older.

The lambs thus carefully chosen were to be slain on the fourteenth day of the month, "in the evening" (12:6). The last phrase is literally "between the two evenings." This is a technical expression which has been interpreted in three different ways: (1) the period between sunset and dark; (2) the period between noon and nightfall; (3) the period between midafternoon and sunset. The last interpretation was the one adopted by the Pharisees, Josephus, and the Talmud.[4] It seems to have determined the time of the slaying of the Passover lambs in the time of Jesus.

Special attention was given to the disposition of the blood of the Passover lamb. Blood was regarded by ancient Hebrews as belonging to God and therefore as especially sacred (see Lev. 1:5; 3:8; 4:5-7). The blood of the Passover lamb was to be smeared on the two doorposts and the lintel of each house where the Israelites were gathered (Ex. 12:7). The doorposts and lintel, because they provided access to a house, were regarded as being especially sacred (see Ex. 21:6; Deut. 6:9). The blood was placed there as a protection against the destroyer when he was sent to smite the firstborn of Egypt (Ex. 12:22-23). When the Lord saw the blood on the doorposts and lintel, he would pass over the door and not allow the destroyer to enter that house.

According to 12:8, the Passover meal consisted of three main ingredients: roasted lamb's meat, unleavened bread, and bitter herbs. Verse 9 specifically forbids the eating of meat that was either raw or boiled in water; it had to be roasted. Later this rule was changed to require that the Passover lamb be boiled (Deut. 16:7). No satisfactory explanation has been given for the variation in this requirement.

The bitter herbs reminded the Israelites of their bitter experience in Egypt. Exodus 1:13-14 reads, "So they made the people of Israel serve with rigor, and made their lives bitter with hard service." The herbs originally were probably the wild desert plants which the nomads gathered to season their food. The Mishnah lists five herbs that could be used to fulfill the Passover requirement: lettuce, chickory, pepperwort, snakeroot, and dandelion.[5]

The manner in which the Passover meal was to be eaten is specified in 12:11. It was to be eaten "in haste." The Hebrew word found here includes the sense of fear as well as haste. Those who ate the Passover were to be ready to march at a moment's notice. The note of urgency can be felt in the instructions they received, " 'In this manner you shall eat it: your loins girded, your sandals on your feet, and your staff in your hand.' "

"To gird the loins" is a very graphic idiom drawn from everyday life in ancient Israel. When Israelite men were relaxing at home, they wore long, flowing robes over their undergarments. However, when they needed to move rapidly, as in battle or on a long journey, they would gather up the skirts of their robes and tuck them under a sash tied around the waist. This permitted them to move freely without tripping over the loose ends of their robes. One who was prepared in this manner for swift action was said to have girded his loins.

The New Testament applies the same idiom to Christian pilgrims. Jesus admonished his disciples to be prepared for his coming in these words, " 'Let your loins be girded and your lamps burning, and be like men who are waiting for their master to come home from the marriage feast, so that they may open to him at once when he comes and

knocks' " (Luke 12:35-36). Paul likewise employed this idiom. He may
even have been thinking of the Passover march of the ancient Hebrews
when he wrote these words to Christians, "Stand therefore, having
girded your loins with truth, and having put on the breastplate of righteousness, and having shod your feet with the equipment of the gospel
of peace" (Eph. 6:14-15). The Christian too is to be ready to march at
a moment's notice.

Exodus 12:11 concludes with the statement, " 'It is the Lord's
passover.' " The Hebrew for Passover is *pesach*. The corresponding
verb, *pasach* (meaning "to pass over") is used in verse 13, " 'When I see
the blood, I will pass over you.' " An entirely different verb, meaning
"to pass through," is used in verse 12. When God "passed through"
Egypt he "passed over" the houses of the Israelites.

The original meaning of *pasach*, "to pass over," and *pesach*,
"Passover," is much debated. The verb occurs in Isaiah 31:5 where it
means "to stand over in order to protect." If this meaning is applied in
Exodus, the Passover becomes a festival celebrating divine protection.
This seems to be about as close as we can come to its original meaning.

Exodus 12:14-20 furnishes more detailed instruction for keeping
the Feast of Unleavened Bread. The first day of this feast was marked
by the removal of all leaven from the house (v. 15). Leaven was simply
a piece of fermented dough kept from a previous batch. Israel's law
codes forbade the offering of sacrifices with leaven (Ex. 23:18; 34:25).
Leaven is often regarded in the Bible as a symbol of corruption (see
Matt. 16:11). Paul interpreted leaven in this sense, as can be seen in his
letter to the Christians in Corinth: "Your boasting is not good. Do you
not know that a little leaven leavens the whole lump? Cleanse out the
old leaven that you may be a new lump, as you really are unleavened.
For Christ, our paschal lamb, has been sacrificed. Let us, therefore,
celebrate the festival, not with the old leaven, the leaven of malice and
evil, but with the unleavened bread of sincerity and truth" (1 Cor.
5:6-8).

Twice in Exodus 12 (vv. 15,19) it is stated that anyone eating leaven
during the seven days of Unleavened Bread was to be "cut off from the
congregation of Israel." This was a harsh measure and was equivalent
to excommunication.

The first day and the final day of the Feast of Unleavened Bread
were regarded as being especially sacred (v. 16). On these two days
holy assemblies were to be held, and no work could be done. The instructions for their observance are practically the same as those for the
sabbath.

Exodus 12:21-28 relates how Moses instructed the elders of Israel to keep the first Passover and how the people responded in reverent submission. There are only one or two new elements in these verses. One is the reference to the use of hyssop for sprinkling the blood of the Passover lamb on the doorposts and lintel (v. 22). Hyssop was a very small, bushy plant, probably to be identified with a modern plant called marjoram. It is referred to in 1 Kings 4:33 as the smallest of all plants, "the hyssop that grows out of the wall."

Another new feature in these instructions is the reference to the destroyer's not being allowed to enter the house of any Israelite to slay the firstborn (Ex. 12:23). Concerning this reference Clements has written: "The destroyer is not more precisely defined, but must be related to the destroying angel mentioned elsewhere in the Old Testament (2 Sam. 24:16; Isa. 37:36). He appears as the agent of God's work and not as a rival to him."[6]

One of the most important points in this passage is the charge to Israelite parents to use the Passover as an occasion for giving religious instruction to their children. Moses said to the elders of Israel, " 'When you come to the land which the Lord will give you, as he has promised, you shall keep this service. And when your children say to you, "What do you mean by this service?" you shall say, "It is the sacrifice of the Lord's passover, for he passed over the houses of the people of Israel in Egypt, when he slew the Egyptians but spared our houses" ' " (Ex. 12:25-27; see also Deut. 4:9; 6:7,20-25; Josh. 4:6-7,20-24).

A basic principle laid down in these verses is that religious instruction is to be given in response to questions raised by the children themselves. Too often those who have tried to teach children have violated this basic principle. They have discouraged children's asking questions. They prefer to question the children. And often the questions the teachers ask are not those for which the children are seeking answers. The better way is for children to be encouraged to ask serious questions about God and about the meaning of life. Parents who honestly and patiently attempt to answer these questions will have many opportunities to lead their children into meaningful learning experiences.

"The people bowed their heads and worshiped" (Ex. 12:27) is this section's concluding statement. It sounds a note of reverent submission. These virtually are the same words used at the end of the account of the first interview between Moses and Aaron and the elders of Israel (Ex. 4:31). This time the people were ready to be led to freedom.

3. Israel's Escape from Egypt (*12:29-42*)

The tenth plague finally fell upon the Egyptians. The Lord went forth at midnight and all the firstborn in the land of Egypt were smitten. The victims of the tenth plague included all the firstborn of the land of Egypt, from the firstborn of Pharaoh to the firstborn of the lowliest servant. Even the firstborn of cattle were smitten. Only the Israelites escaped.

A mighty cry went up from the land of Egypt at midnight (v. 30). Every Egyptian household which had a son was plunged into mourning. Even the royal palace was not exempt from the grief.

Pharaoh had earlier vowed that Moses would never see his face again (Ex. 10:28). The tenth plague made him take back his words and summon Moses and Aaron to come before him. He did this on the very night his firstborn was slain. He was afraid to delay another moment for fear some worse evil would strike him. The first clauses in verses 29,30, and 31 all end in the word "night": "At midnight" (v. 29); "Pharaoh rose up in the night" (v. 30); "He summoned Moses and Aaron by night" (v. 31). The effect of this repetition is to stress the feeling of terror that hovered over Egypt on that fateful night. In their Hebrew form, verses 31 and 32 are written mainly in short, terse words of only one or two syllables each. This also heightens the dramatic sense of the passage. It suggests that Pharaoh was seized with a nameless dread and fear as he begged Moses and Aaron to lead the Israelites out of Egypt with all haste.

Verse 32 ends with a unique request. As Pharaoh bade Moses and Aaron leave his land, he requested of them, " 'Bless me also!' " Centuries earlier Jacob had entered Egypt and had blessed the Pharaoh on the occasion of their first meeting (Gen. 47:7,10). On the night of the Exodus during his last meeting with the descendants of Jacob, the later Pharaoh also requested a blessing. There is more to this request than meets the eye. It serves as a reminder of the promise made centuries earlier to Abraham, "I will bless those who bless you, and him who curses you I will curse; and by you all the families of the earth shall be blessed" (Gen. 12:3; author's translation). When Pharaoh requested a blessing from Moses and Aaron, it was an indication that Abraham's power to bless the nations had been passed on to them and to the people they were leading to freedom. The promises to the patriarchs were being renewed in their day. They now knew that they were the true descendants of Abraham and heirs of the promises of God.

The number of the Israelites who left Egypt is given in Exodus 12:37 as six hundred thousand men, besides women and children. Honeycutt has proposed an interpretation of this statement that is based on the research of George Mendenhall.[7] Mendenhall has demonstrated that the Hebrew word *'eleph,* translated "thousand," may also mean "clan," or "family," that is, a subsection of a tribal group. Such groupings were for the purpose of military service. Applied to Exodus 12:37, this may mean that Moses led out of Egypt six hundred military units, totaling perhaps two thousand five hundred men, or a combined total including women and children, that ranged from twelve to twenty-five thousand persons.[8]

According to Exodus 12:40-41, the time that the people of Israel dwelt in Egypt was 430 years. Exodus 6:16-20 states that four generations covered the span from Levi to Moses. Since 430 years appear to be a period longer than that required by four generations, Old Testament interpreters have sought an explanation. One solution to this difficulty is suggested by the Septuagint's rendering of Exodus 12:40, "The sojourning of the children of Israel, while they sojourned in the land of Egypt and the land of Chanaan [*sic*], was four hundred and thirty years."[9] This version allows for two periods of equal length, the first covering the sojourn in Canaan and the second covering that in Egypt. This interpretation is supported by the Samaritan Pentateuch, the Old Latin, Josephus, and the New Testament (Gal. 3:17). Josephus is very specific, "They left Egypt . . . four hundred and thirty years after our forefather Abraham came into Canaan, but two hundred and fifteen years only after Jacob removed into Egypt."[10] Paul in Galatians 3:17 says that the law was given at Sinai 430 years after the call of Abraham. According to that, the 430 years span the wanderings in Canaan and the sojourn in Egypt.

Exodus 12:42 designates the night of the Passover as a "night of watching" or "a night of vigil" to be kept by the people of Israel throughout their generations. The verse makes a play on the word *shamar,* which means not only "to watch" but also "to keep, preserve, protect." Passover is both a night of watching "by the Lord" and a night of watching kept "to the Lord." It was a night of watching from Israel's side and a night of protecting from the Lord's side. As Israel watched for the Lord, the Lord watched over Israel. From this passage has come the custom of observing "watch night" services in our churches.

4. Additional Regulations for Keeping Passover *(12:43 to 13:10)*
Passover and the Feast of Unleavened Bread were to be observed not just once but year by year throughout all generations. In this way all

future Israelites would be reminded of the central event at the beginning of their history. They would also relive history as they reenacted the essential elements of the celebration of the first Passover in Egypt. Israelites living long after this event were taught to say, "Every man in every generation is bound to look upon himself as if he personally had gone forth from Egypt. . . . It is not only our fathers that the Holy One redeemed, but ourselves also did He redeem with them. For does not the Scripture say: And He brought *us* out thence that He might bring *us* in, to give *us* the land which He swore unto our fathers (Deuteronomy 6:23)?"[11]

Exodus 12:43-49 deals primarily with the question of who may be admitted to the celebration of Passover. Verse 43 excludes from participation the foreigner who chances to be in the land of Israel. However, the sojourner in the land, that is, the foreigner who has taken up permanent residence, may partake of the Passover, provided he and all male members of his household have been circumcised (v. 48). Such sojourners generally enjoyed the same rights and were subject to the same regulations as the Israelites (see Lev. 19:34; 22:18; 24:16; Num. 35:15).

Verses 46-47 stress the idea of unity in the celebration of the Passover. It was to be eaten in one house (v. 46; see also Ex. 12:22). It was to be roasted whole, not even a bone of it being broken (v. 46; see also Ex. 12:9). Verse 46 is quoted in John 19:36 and applied to the crucifixion of Jesus. Finally, the Passover was to be kept by all the congregation of Israel (v. 47).

5. The Law of the Firstborn *(13:1,11-16)*

Ancient Israelites believed that the firstborn of both men and animals possessed a sanctity that made them uniquely the property of God. Therefore that which first came from the womb among the people of Israel or among their flocks and herds was to be consecrated (v. 1) and set apart to the Lord (v. 12). This apparently meant that the firstborn were to be brought to the priests to be offered up in sacrifice. A similar requirement was made with regard to the firstfruits of the harvest (see Ex. 22:29; Deut. 26:1-11).

Since the Israelites did not practice child sacrifice, provision had to be made for the redemption of their firstborn sons. This was effected by the payment of a special redemption price for their lives (Ex. 13:13). The redemption price for a firstborn son is not stated in this passage. At a later time the consecration of the Levites to the Lord was regarded as a substitution for the offering of all the firstborn sons of the Israelites to the Lord (see Num. 8:14-18). Unclean animals, because they were unsuitable to be offered in sacrifice to the Lord, were also to be redeemed (Ex. 13:13; Lev. 27:26-27; Num. 18:15-16).

The New English Bible translates Exodus 13:16, " 'You shall have the record of it as a sign upon your hand, and upon your forehead as a phylactery, because by the strength of his hand the Lord brought us out of Egypt.' " The Jews of later times took these instructions, along with those of Deuteronomy 6:8 and 11:18, quite literally. They made cubicle leather boxes called phylacteries. These were worn on the forehead and on the left arm (see Matt. 23:5). The phylacteries contained small pieces of parchment on which were written the following passages: Exodus 13:1-10,11-16; Deut. 6:4-9; 11:13-21. The phylacteries were worn especially at the time of the daily morning prayer.

6. Lessons for Life from the Scriptures

As we conclude our study of the plagues, we should be careful not to draw wrong conclusions from them. We must not suppose that America or any other modern nation stands as a chosen nation before God as Israel did in the Old Testament. God has not made a covenant with our nation to protect it against other nations. God's love and concern extends to all nations, and we must never suppose that he is the enemy of our enemies.

Honeycutt has given an excellent summary statement on the significance of the plagues for the faith of Israel: "The theology of the plague narratives assumes that they were revelatory in nature and character; that they revealed a God who was unique, incomparable, powerful, and to be known among the nations through his actions in history. He was the sovereign Lord of creation, who delivered his people in the midst of calamity and who was victorious over all powers hostile to his purposes, even the gods of Egypt. In essence, the plagues demonstrate that Yahweh, God of Israel, is Lord of creation."[12]

Christian parents should be equally as diligent as the ancient Hebrews were in providing their young with religious instruction. It has been said that the world is always just one generation removed from paganism. If the present generation of Christians does not pass on the spiritual heritage it has received, then this heritage will be destroyed. The task of religious instruction is not optional. It is a must in every generation.

Christian parents should be as willing as the ancient Hebrews were to dedicate their children to God. Not only firstborn sons but all children of Christian parents should be regarded as gifts from the Lord to be consecrated to him. The vocations young people choose, the style of their living, and their choice of a life companion would be greatly influenced if they had a sense of belonging to God. It is sad but true that some parents gladly offer their children to their country or to some lesser good but withhold them from God. When did we last pray that God would take our sons and our daughters and use them for his glory?

The New Testament emphasizes the Christian significance of the Passover. In the days of Herod's Temple, Passover had become virtually the feast of the coming messiah. There was a general expectation among the Jews that messiah would appear in Jerusalem during the Passover celebration. This caused the Romans to double the military guard in Jerusalem during this season.

And Messiah did appear! John's Gospel is the one that most forcefully presents the Passover symbolism. It describes Jesus' ministry as structured around a series of religious festivals: Passover (2:12,23); an unidentified feast (5:1); Passover (6:4); Tabernacles (7:2,37); Dedication (10:22); and Passover (11:55; 12:1; 13:1; 18:28,39; 19:14). Three Passover celebrations are included here, one at the beginning of Jesus' ministry, one at the middle, and one at the end. The one at the end receives the most attention.

This structuring of Jesus' ministry around Passover festivals has not only chronological but also theological significance. In fact, the entire Gospel of John has a Passover character. It begins with one Passover and ends with another. In the beginning it hails Jesus as the Lamb of God (1:36). In the end it pictures him as being crucified on the afternoon of the day of preparation of the Passover (19:14,31,42). This was the day when pious Jews carried their Passover lambs to the Temple to be slain. At the very hour the lambs were being slain in the Temple, the Son of God was slain upon a cross. " 'Behold, the Lamb of God, who takes away the sin of the world!' " (John 1:29).

Childs[13] has listed three ways in which Passover links the Exodus from Egypt with God's redemption in Jesus Christ: (1) the Passover bears witness that God is interested in man's physical bondage as well as his spiritual bondage; (2) the Passover emphasizes the collective nature of the community of the redeemed—God redeemed a people for his own; (3) Passover stresses the future hope of God's people. Even though Egypt lay behind the Israelites, an even greater redemption awaited them in the future. And when we celebrate the Lord's Supper, our Passover memorial, it is that we might proclaim his sacrificial death *until he comes again* (see 1 Cor. 5:6-8; 11:23-26; Rev. 5:6-14).

---

[1]Ronald E. Clements, *Exodus,* The Cambridge Bible Commentary (Cambridge: Cambridge University Press, 1972), p. 65.

[2]Flavius Josephus, *The Works of Flavius Josephus,* trans. William Whiston, Vol. 1 (Nashville: Broadman Press, 1974), VI. ix. 3.

[3]A. Cohen, *The Soncino Chumash* (Hindhead, Surrey: The Soncino Press, 1947), p. 387.

[4]J. Philip Hyatt, *Exodus,* New Century Bible (London: Oliphants, 1971), p. 132.

[5]Childs, *op. cit.,* p. 182.

[6]Clements, *op. cit.,* p. 73.

[7]Roy L. Honeycutt, Jr., *The Broadman Bible Commentary,* Vol. 1 (Nashville: Broadman Press, 1969), pp. 350-51.

[8]See also Gabriel Hebert, *When Israel Came Out of Egypt* (London: SCM Press, Ltd., 1961), pp. 82-83.

[9]Septuagint: The Greek translation of the Old Testament from Hebrew. It was translated about 200 B.C. for the whole Greek Empire, whose people, including the Jews, had now adopted Greek as their common language.

[10]Josephus, *op. cit.,* Vol. 2, II. xv. 2.

[11]Theodor H. Gaster, *Passover: Its History and Traditions* (Boston: Beacon Press, 1962), p. 63.

[12]Honeycutt, *op. cit.,* p. 354.

[13]Childs, *op. cit.,* pp. 213-14.

Personal Learning Activities

1. The despoiling of the Egyptians has been explained in the textbook as (select one):
   ____ (1) A clever ruse the Israelites used on the Egyptians.
   ____ (2) An act of divine justice under covenant law.
   ____ (3) A plain fraud.
2. From the list of statements below select those applicable to Passover:
   ____ (1) The oldest continuously observed religious festival known to mankind.
   ____ (2) Observed first on the eve of the Exodus.
   ____ (3) A family-centered festival.
   ____ (4) A lamb (or goat) used as sacrificial animal, without blemish, and within the year of its birth.
   ____ (5) The sacrificial animal's blood applied on the lintel and doorposts of the observers' home.
   ____ (6) Observed with the loins girded to indicate preparation for travel.
   ____ (7) A festival celebrating divine protection.
3. Identify elements of Passover that relate to Christ's atoning work, and state the relationship.
4. The observance of the Feast of Unleavened Bread and Passover, according to Exodus 13 (see v. 14), served as a device for teaching basic facts of Israel's faith to the children of each succeeding generation. Recently we passed through the observance of another Christmas. How does the principle of using a religious festival to teach children basic facts about one's religious faith relate to Christmas? How can Christmas be used to teach children these facts? What changes in your family's observance of Christmas would be required to make it conform to this principle?

———

Answers:

1. (2); 2. All responses; 3. Your answer; 4. Your answer.

5

God Makes a Way

Exodus 13:17 to 15:21

The book of Exodus may be divided into six sections: (1) the oppression of the Israelites in Egypt (1:1-22); (2) preparations for deliverance (2:1 to 6:30); (3) the ten plagues in Egypt (7:1 to 13:16); (4) the Exodus from Egypt and the crossing of the sea (13:17 to 15:21); (5) the journey from the sea to Mount Sinai (15:22 to 18:27); (6) events and laws at Mount Sinai (19:1 to 40:38).

Careful attention to this outline will make clear that the salvation recorded in Exodus 13:17 to 15:21 was climactic and decisive. This involved the actual Exodus out of Egypt and the crossing of the sea. These events acquired greater and greater significance as time went on. They were regarded by Israel as the Lord's mightiest acts of salvation and redemption. Israel escaped from Egypt to the accompaniment of events so stupendous that they were impressed forever on her memory. These events were memorialized in Israel's earliest creeds (see Deut. 6:21-23; 26:8; Josh. 24:6-7; 1 Sam. 12:6). And from early times to late they were celebrated in song (see Pss. 66:1-7; 74:12-17; 77:11-20; 89:8-10; 106:6-12; 114:1-8; 136:10-15). However one may arrange the materials in Exodus 1-15, they reach their culmination and grand finale in the song of victory recorded in chapter 15.

Exodus 1-15 begins with a cry of distress (2:23) and ends with a shout of praise (15:18). After the miraculous deliverance at the sea the Israelites set out for Sinai with a song in their hearts. They had something to celebrate, something to sing about. They sang the Lord's praises in these words, " 'I will sing to the Lord, for he has triumphed gloriously;/the horse and his rider he has thrown into the sea' " (15:1).

The poem introduced by these words has probably an ancient Passover cantata, sung by successive generations of Israelites as they celebrated the birth of their freedom.

The Lord effected a great deliverance at the Red Sea. But he effected an even greater deliverance at Calvary. Christians are heirs and beneficiaries of both of these victories. This is beautifully set forth in Revelation 15:2-4. The writer of Revelation saw the saints of God in anticipation of the final victory, singing praises to God for his righteous judgment. This ransomed multitude also stood beside a sea, in this instance a sea of glass mingled with fire (Rev. 15:2). In their hands they had harps (Rev. 15:2), reminding us of the timbrels after Israel's deliverance from the Red Sea (Ex. 15:20). The conquered beast (Rev. 15:2) is paralleled by the defeated army of the Egyptians.

The victorious multitude beside the sea of glass sang the song of Moses *and* the song of the Lamb (Rev. 15:3). The song beside the Red Sea was but the prelude to that song beside the sea of glass. The first celebrated the victory of Moses, the second the victory of the Lamb. The first victory song proclaimed that the Lord would reign forever and ever (Ex. 15:18); the second proclaimed him "King of the ages" (Rev. 15:3). The first victory caused Israel to believe in the Lord (Ex. 14:31); the second victory will result in all nations bowing before him in praise and adoration (Rev. 15:4). God be praised for his great and wonderful deeds!

1. The Journey from Succoth to the Sea *(13:17 to 14:4)*
The first day's journey took the Israelites as far as Succoth (Ex. 12:37). This first stopping place on the road to freedom is probably to be identified with modern Tell el-Maskhuta. At Succoth the Israelites were still within the territory of Egypt.

The second day of their journey took the Israelites from Succoth to Etham, which is said to have been situated "on the edge of the wilderness" (Ex. 13:20; see also Num. 33:6,8). It was probably an Egyptian fortress lying on the border of the land to the east of Succoth.

It is impossible to trace the route of the Exodus from this point with any certainty. All that is known for a fact is that the Israelites left Egypt from the north, passed somewhere between the Gulf of Suez and the Mediterranean Sea, and went into the Wilderness of Shur (Ex. 13:17-18; 15:22).

According to Exodus 13:17, God did not lead the Israelites through the territory of the Philistines, lest war break out and they become discouraged. The Philistines were a people who came from the Aegean area by way of the sea. For this reason they were sometimes referred to as "the sea people." They settled in the coastal plains of the land of Canaan after unsuccessful attempts to invade Egypt. Because of them the name of the land was later changed from Canaan to Palestine. Their main settlements in Canaan took place around 1200 B.C., roughly the same time as the Exodus.

The main military route from Egypt to Canaan crossed the territory of the Philistines. If the Israelites had gone that way, they would have required no more than ten days to reach their destination. Instead, God led them the longer route past Mount Sinai. The implication of Exodus 13:17 is that the Philistines would have attacked them if they had taken the shorter route through their land.

"God led the people round by the way of the wilderness toward the Red Sea" (Ex. 13:18). "Red Sea" is a translation based not upon Hebrew but upon the Greek translation of the Old Testament. The Hebrew reads *yam suph,* "sea of reeds." Most likely this was not the Red Sea itself, but a body of water farther north. The crossing of the sea probably took place at Lake Timsah in northern Egypt. The body of water in question had to be fairly near the cities from which the Israelites had escaped, since they seem to have reached it in two or three days. As a matter of fact, the exact identification of the body of water is of little importance. The significant fact is that God wrought a great deliverance for Israel when it appeared that there was no possible way of escape.

The latter part of verse 13:18 is rendered, "The people of Israel went up out of the land of Egypt equipped for battle." *The New English Bible* reads, "The fifth generation of Israelites departed from Egypt." This rendering is permitted by the Hebrew and may be better suited to the context. Whichever translation is used, the text makes clear that the Lord fought the Egyptians for the Hebrews (14:13-14, 15:3).

The Israelites took the bones of Joseph with them as they left Egypt (Ex. 13:19). This was in keeping with the request of the dying patriarch many years before the Exodus took place (see Gen. 50:25-26). Joseph's faith that the Israelites would someday return to Canaan was now being vindicated.

The Lord went before his people in a pillar of cloud by day and a pillar of fire by night (Ex. 13:21-22). This may reflect the ancient custom of carrying a burning brazier at the head of a marching army to indicate the line of march by day and by night.

According to Exodus 14:1-2, God commanded the hosts of Israel to turn back and to encamp before Pi-ha-hiroth. Apparently the Israelites had been unable to break through the border defenses at Etham (see 13:20). Their turning back led Pharaoh to suppose that they had lost their way and were wandering aimlessly in the land (Ex. 14:3). Thus the stage was set for the final climactic confrontation between Pharaoh's army and the God of Israel.

2. Pharaoh Pursues the Israelites *(14:5-20)*

Six points are made clear in Exodus 14:5 to 15:21:

1. The Israelites were hopelessly trapped between the sea and the army of Pharaoh (14:5-9).
2. The Lord was present on the side of Israel.
   His presence is shown in various ways.
   a. The Lord acted through Moses, his representative (14:15-16).
   b. He accompanied Israel in the form of the angel of God (14:19).
   c. He was present in the pillar of cloud and fire (14:24).
3. God opened a way through the sea and provided a means of escape for his people.
   God used two means to accomplish this.
   a. He instructed Moses to stretch out his rod over the sea, and the waters were divided (14:16,21,26-27).
   b. God caused an east wind to blow all night and drive back the waters of the sea (14:21; 15:8,10).
4. The enemies of Israel were destroyed in the sea.
   This is stated in various ways.
   a. The Lord confused them and caused their chariots to become mired in the mud (14:24-25).
   b. Moses stretched out his hand, and the sea returned to cover them (14:26-28).
   c. The Lord threw Pharaoh's chariots and all his host into the sea, where they sank like a stone (15:1,4-5,21).
5. Israel experienced a great deliverance (14:30).
6. By means of this mighty act Israel "believed in the Lord" (14:31), and the nations were forced to acknowledge the power of the Lord (14:4,17-18; 15:14-16).

The drowning of the Egyptians in the heart of the sea is presented almost as if it were an eleventh plague. As in the other ten plagues, it was the hardening of Pharaoh's heart that set the stage for his encounter with God (14:4-5,17). And as in the other plagues, Pharaoh came out the loser. In spite of his overwhelming superiority in military strength, he was unable to prevent the Israelites' escaping into the wilderness. All his efforts to stop them only served to show his powerlessness before the Lord and the utter helplessness of his gods.

The Egyptians' use of war chariots, a practice they had inherited from the Hyksos, made a deep impression on the Israelites (14:6-7, 17-18,23). Israel did not begin to make use of horses and chariots in its own army until the reign of Solomon. The fact that the Egyptians were so well equipped and still failed to recapture the departing Israelites was further proof of the superior power of Israel's God.

When the Israelites saw the Egyptians coming after them and realized that there was only a sea in front of them, they were in great fear (14:10). They cried out to the Lord. The Hebrew word translated "to cry out" always means to cry out because of great distress. Their reaction demonstrated the weakness of their faith. It is easier to take people out of slavery than to take slavery out of people. The long, bitter years of Egyptian bondage had rendered the Israelites servile and cowardly. They already longed for the security that they had enjoyed in Egypt (14:11-12). It is important to recognize that precisely at the moment when Israel's future was the darkest and her faith the weakest, God chose to perform his mightiest act of deliverance.

There is a note of bitter irony in the question addressed to Moses in Exodus 14:11, " 'Is it because there are no graves in Egypt that you have taken us away to die in the wilderness?' " Of course there were graves in Egypt! Egypt was famous for her giant pyramid tombs. Israel's cry of distress and her bitter complaint against Moses only served to magnify her lack of faith. They would rather live out their lives in servility in Egypt and die there than die prematurely in the wilderness. The faith of the Israelites did not produce the miracle of deliverance. Rather, the miracle of deliverance gave birth to the faith of his people. In the end all the glory and all the credit for the great deliverance belonged to God alone.

Moses' response to the doubting multitude of Israelites is one of the greatest calls to faith to be found anywhere in the Scriptures: " 'Fear not, stand firm, and see the salvation of the Lord, which he will work for you today; for the Egyptians whom you see today, you shall never see again. The Lord will fight for you, and you have only to be still' "

(14:13-14).

Walter Harrelson has written of this moment in Israel's experience with penetrating insight:

> The remarkable fact about this event is that Moses rests his case entirely with Yahweh. The people are hopelessly trapped. There is no way out for them, no matter what they do. But Moses calls for them to stand firm, and see what Yahweh will do! This is precisely the quality of faith which the prophet Isaiah later on portrays with great vividness: complete trust in Yahweh, no matter what the consequences. It is the sort of faith depicted in the story of Abraham's readiness to offer Isaac to Yahweh. . . . The event beside the sea would have been of no consequence at all, we may be sure, had there not been such an affirmation of faith. What makes this culminating event in the Exodus story of such profound importance for the community of Israel is the presence of this readiness to lay one's life before God and live or die in dependence upon Him. . . . Israelite faith . . . received its supreme test when all hope was lost and yet Moses hoped and trusted in the God who would save His people.[1]

In the experience at the sea the Lord came to his people as Warrior, Conqueror, and Victor. Moses told the trembling multitude, " 'The Lord will fight for you, and you have only to be still' " (14:14). After the Egyptians had been destroyed in the sea, the Israelites sang boldly, " 'The Lord is a man of war; / the Lord is his name' " (15:3). When Miriam and all the women went out with timbrels and dancing and singing, they reflected the ancient custom of women going out to meet returning warriors and welcoming them with songs of triumph (15:20-21). In this instance, however, it was not Israel's army that had won a victory, but the Lord of hosts himself. His power had prevailed against the hostile forces of history (Pharaoh and his army) and of nature (the sea).

The "holy war" motif is especially prominent in the early books of the Old Testament. There are six features of this motif present in the story of the destruction of the Egyptians in the waters of the sea: (1) The people of God were threatened by a vastly superior army, causing them to cry out in distress (Ex. 14:5-12; see Judg. 4:1-3); (2) the people were reassured that God was able to deliver them (Ex. 14:13-14; see Josh. 10:8; Judg. 4:14); (3) the people were commanded to go forward (Ex. 14:15; see Josh. 8:1-2; Judg. 6:14); (4) the Lord intervened on behalf of his people (Ex. 14:21-25; see Josh. 10:11; Judg. 4:15); (5) the enemy was terrified and laid prostrate by the Lord (Ex. 14:24-25; see Josh. 10:10; Judg. 7:20-22); (6) the people were careful to give the Lord full credit for the victory (Ex. 15:1-21; see Judg. 5:1-31).

This additional word concerning holy war comes from Clements: "Primarily such 'holy' wars were defensive, although not exclusively so, and required special regulations to ensure the proper dedication of Israel's soldiers, and to ensure that all credit for the victory was accorded to God, to whom all the spoil was devoted. God fought for Israel by using the forces of nature to assist his people, and by instilling panic in the enemy. Cp. Exod. 17:8-16; Josh. 10:12-13; Judg. 5:19-23."[2]

3. The Crossing of the Sea *(14:21-31)*

The crossing of the sea illustrates God's majestic power and the gracious manner in which he deals with his people. He often closes up all normal avenues of escape in order to demonstrate his power to deliver. In such situations we discover with the prophet of old that it is "not by might, nor by power, but by my Spirit, says the Lord of hosts" (Zech. 4:6). The Exodus account stresses that Israel's deliverance was wrought by God alone. He provided a way of escape when there was no hope left. He did the impossible, dividing the sea and defeating the most powerful nation on earth, thus bringing to birth a new nation. That such a nation should emerge from the jaws of death was a singular demonstration of divine grace and power. Is it any wonder that Israel's faith in God as Redeemer was born out of this experience?

The motif of the parting of the waters is prominent elsewhere in the Old Testament. At creation God separated the waters, established the firmament (Gen. 1:6-7), and divided the waters from the dry land (Gen. 1:9-10). When the Israelites entered Canaan, the Jordan was stopped in order that they might cross over on dry land (Josh. 3:14-17). Elijah and Elisha each parted the waters of the Jordan and crossed on dry land (2 Kings 2:8,14). Isaiah prophesied that God would deliver his people from exile in Assyria by a miracle similar to that at the Red Sea (Isa. 11:15-16).

The significant point in each of these passages is that God makes a way for his people not *around* but *through* all sorts of obstacles and difficulties. This is beautifully expressed in Isaiah 43:1-2: "Thus says the Lord, who created you, O Jacob, he who formed you, O Israel:

'Fear not, for I have redeemed you; I have called you by name, you are mine. When you pass through the waters I will be with you; and through the rivers, they shall not overwhelm you; when you walk through fire you shall not be burned, and the flame shall not consume you.' " God makes a way even though his people can find none.

Another motif that is prominent in chapters 14 and 15 is that of the sea. The word "sea" occurs no less than sixteen times in chapter 14. In 15:1-21 such terms as "sea," "Red Sea," "floods," "depths," "waters," "deeps," "mighty waters," and "waters of the sea" are found a total of fifteen times. The sea is often regarded in the Scriptures as a threatening force, an enemy to be conquered. At creation God gathered the waters into seas (Gen. 1:10) and fixed a boundary that their waves might not pass (Job 38:8-11; Ps. 104:6-7). The psalmist addressed the sea as if it were a living force and taunted it for having fled from the Lord at the Exodus (Ps. 114:1-6). Hostility toward the sea is carried over into the New Testament. Revelation 21:1 foresaw a time when the sea would be abolished, "Then I saw a new heaven and a new earth; for the first heaven and the first earth had passed away, and the sea was no more." This is but another way of saying that God will eventually bring under his control all forces that are hostile toward him.

With the crossing of the Red Sea the question again arises regarding the relation between natural and supernatural in the event. On the one hand, it is stated that Moses was told to stretch out his hand over the sea and divide it (14:16). On the other hand, we are told that a strong east wind blew all night and drove back the sea (14:21).

Childs has shown that the natural and supernatural elements in this event cannot really be separated:

> Again, the deliverance at the sea was effected by a combination of the wonderful and the ordinary. The waters were split by the rod of Moses, but a strong wind blew all night and laid bare the sea bed. The waters stood up as a mighty wall to the left and the right, and yet the Egyptians were drowned when the sea returned to its normal channels. Yahweh produced panic with his fiery glance, but it was the mud of the sea bottom which clogged the wheels of the heavy chariots. The elements of the wonderful and the ordinary are constitutive to the greatest of Old Testament events. There never was a time when the event was only understood as ordinary, nor was there a time when the supernatural absorbed the natural.

But Israel saw the mighty hand of God at work in both the ordinary and the wonderful, and never sought to fragment the great act of redemption into parts.[3]

Just when the Israelites appeared to be hopelessly trapped between the sea and the pursuing Egyptians, God made a way for them through the sea (14:22). However, the way of escape for the Israelites became the way of destruction for their pursuers. This remarkable triumph remained in the memory of Israel as a classic example of what the salvation of the Lord means. It means that the Lord is able to overrule events and adverse circumstances to bring deliverance to those who trust in him. A later psalm celebrating God's power to deliver his people includes this declaration of faith, "Surely the wrath of men shall praise thee; the residue of wrath thou wilt gird upon thee" (Ps. 76:10).

A comparison should be made between Exodus 14:25 and 5:9. The same Hebrew root signifying "heaviness" occurs in both these passages. When the Israelites asked permission to leave Egypt and go a three-day journey into the wilderness to serve their God, Pharaoh made their work load *heavier*. And when the Egyptians sought to cross the sea in pursuit of the fleeing Israelites, God clogged the wheels of the Egyptian chariots so that they lumbered along *heavily*. There was a grim justice at work at the sea. Egypt was reaping as she had sown.

The theologically significant word "to save" appears in 14:30. It is found also in Exodus 2:17, but there Moses is the subject and it is translated "to help." Exodus 14:30 is the first instance in the Old Testament where this verb is used with God as the subject. It is said here that God "saved" Israel that day from the hand of the Egyptians.

The basic meaning of the Hebrew verb "to save" is "to be wide, spacious, free." In the broadest sense of the term, salvation means freedom. In the context of the Exodus it refers to the deliverance of the Israelites from bondage and death. This should remind us that God is concerned for the physical freedom of men. Where men are enslaved by oppression, ignorance, disease, or hunger, God is concerned that they be free. But he is no less concerned with the need for release from spiritual bondage. This is why he sent his Son to be our Savior. Jesus said, " 'If the Son makes you free, you will be free indeed' " (John 8:36). Those who know Jesus as Savior and Lord have entered into the glorious liberty of the sons of God. It is they who know the deeper meaning of freedom (see Acts 13:38-39).

In commenting on Exodus 14:30-31, Plastaras has drawn an interesting comparison between these verses and 14:10-12:

Thus is described the 'conversion' of Israel. In 14:1-12, . . . the Israelites had *seen* the Egyptians and *feared* (v. 10), and had refused to believe either in Moses or in Yahweh, complaining, 'What have you done to us, in bringing us out of Egypt?' Here on the morning after, Israel again *sees* and *fears,* but now it is Yahweh whom they fear, and they begin to believe in Yahweh and in his spokesman Moses. Up until this moment, Israel's only response to Yahweh's action has been hesitation, murmuring, and disbelief. It is only at this moment that the faith of the people is born. For the first time as a people, they praise the God who has saved them.[4]

4. A Faith That Sings *(15:1-21)*

The prose account of the crossing of the sea is followed by a hymn of praise celebrating the event. Both chapters 14 and 15 state clearly that Israel was not saved because of her faith. In fact, her people failed to believe right up to the last moment. Therefore Israel's faith did not provide the grounds of her salvation. Neither does our faith provide the ground of our salvation. Even faith itself is a gift of God (see Eph. 2:8-9). And yet deliverance calls for a response of faith. And that is what we find in chapter 15. Israel broke out in praise to God and we hear the glad song of the redeemed. The sign of the redeemed of all ages is that they are given "a new song" (see Isa. 52:7-9).

The hymn in chapter 15 is like the rainbow after the storm. Rhodes has written: "What a relief! A song, paean of praise, after fourteen chapters of intense and dramatic action!—This is poetry—folk poetry—the kind of poetry that sticks in one's memory and is sung around the campfire, or on the trail, or in a commemorative worship service. Yet it is poetry grounded in history; it brings to mind something that happened; it dramatizes an event."[5]

The song of Moses (15:1-18) may be outlined as follows: (1) opening hymn of praise (vv. 1-3); (2) celebration of the victory at the sea (vv. 4-10); (3) a second hymn of praise (vv. 11-12); (4) celebration of the safe journey to Canaan and the entry into the land (vv. 13-17); (5) concluding hymn of praise (v. 18).

The opening hymn of praise in verses 1-3 contains Israel's earliest theology in a nutshell. Its theme is not the people of the Exodus but the God of the Exodus. Note the accumulation of divine names in these verses: "Lord," "Lord," "my God," "my father's God," "Lord," "Lord." Note also the parallel descriptive titles: "My strength," "my song," "my salvation," "man of war." Faced with such a God as this, the writer uses several verbs of intent: "I will sing," "I will praise him," "I will exalt him."

In the celebration of the victory at the sea (vv. 4-10), the Lord is pictured as a warrior. In a series of bold images, he is pictured as personally casting his enemies into the sea (v. 4), as shattering the enemy with deadly blows (v. 6), and as breathing out fury like a fire (vv. 7-8).

This vivid description of the destruction of the Egyptians is followed by a second anthem of praise to the Lord (vv. 11-12). The questions in verse 11 presuppose a negative response. There is no other god like the Lord, "majestic in holiness, terrible in glorious deeds, doing wonders" (see Isa. 40:12-26). He stands without a peer among the gods.

The representation of God changes in verses 13-17. He is no longer pictured as a warrior but as a shepherd who gently leads his flock. Israel is led into the Promised Land as in a great procession. Thus the image of war is replaced by the image of peace.

It is to be noted that the movement in the song of Moses is from the past to the future, from past memories to future expectations. The thought passes from the perils of the sea (vv. 4-10) to safe conduct through the desert and into the security and peace of the sanctuary in Jerusalem (vv. 13-17).

Verses 13-17 make clear that the goal of Israel was not the other side of the Red Sea but the land of Canaan. The manner in which God led his people toward this goal is fittingly described in verse 13. Like a shepherd he led them in his love and guided them in his strength. The verb translated "to guide" is found elsewhere in the Old Testament in such passages as Psalm 23:2, "He leads me beside still waters," and Isaiah 40:11, "He will . . . gently lead those that are with young." In the Exodus experience God assumed the role of shepherd to his people.

When the Lord became shepherd, however, he did not change his role as defender of his people. The common theme in verses 4-10 and 13-17 of the song of Moses is the safe passage through threatening dangers to a successful goal. When the Israelites passed through the sea, they were threatened by the Egyptians. And in their passage from the sea to Canaan they were threatened by the Philistines, the Edomites, the Moabites, and the Canaanites (15:14-15).

In both instances the Lord led his people safely through the danger zone. In the first instance they were pursued by the enemy; in the second they were surrounded by the enemy. But in both instances, the Lord acted to nullify the power of the enemy. The first enemy sank

" 'like a stone' " (15:5); the second enemy became still " 'as a stone' " (15:16). Lohfink has described the second group of enemies in these words, "They stand alongside the processional route of Israel like stone sphinxes, and are no more than witnesses to the might of the God of Israel."[6]

For " 'the people whom thou hast redeemed' " (15:13), *The New English Bible* reads, "Whom thou didst ransom." The phrase used here has reference to the freeing of slaves by the payment of their purchase price. In a symbolic sense this is what God did when he secured the release of the Israelites from their bondage in Egypt. Verse 16 refers to the Israelites as " 'the people . . . whom thou hast purchased.' " Here *The New English Bible* reads, "The people whom thou madest thy own." God's deliverance of Israel from Egypt established his lordship over them in a unique way. They were henceforth his, both by right of creation and by right of purchase. In a similar way Christians belong to God as the new Israel. Paul could write to the church at Corinth: "You are not your own; you were bought with a price. So glorify God in your body" (1 Cor. 6:19-20).

The ultimate goal toward which God was leading his people was Mount Zion (vv. 13,17). Various terms are used to designate the place of the Lord's abode with his people. It is called " 'thy holy abode' " (v. 13), " 'thy own mountain' " (v. 17), " 'the place . . . which thou hast made for thy abode' " (v. 17), and " 'the sanctuary . . . which thy hands have established' " (v. 17).

The song affirms that God will " 'plant' " his people on his own mountain (v. 17). These words express stability and permanence. They also express the thought that the settlement of Israel upon Mount Zion is to be regarded as the consummation of God's purpose for her. If this is true, then Israel's true destiny was to become a worshiping community. She was to be planted on the sacred mountain of God's abode where she could continually offer praise and service to him who lives and reigns forever and ever (v. 18). Her true destiny was to glorify her Redeemer and to abide in his presence forever.

The song of Moses is concluded with a hymn celebrating the Lord's rule over his people, " 'The Lord will reign for ever and ever.' " This refrain is found often in the Psalms (for example, Pss. 93:1; 96:10). It suggests that the song of Moses was also designed for use in Temple worship. It was probably sung whenever the Jews gathered in Jerusalem to celebrate the Passover. For this reason it has been designated a Passover cantata.

5. Lessons for Life from the Scriptures

Because Israel's crossing of the Red Sea was a demonstration of divine love and power, it continues to speak with relevance to our generation.

Israel's crossing of the Red Sea tells us that our God is Lord of creation and Lord of history. Just as he opened a way through the sea and overthrew the forces of Pharaoh, so he overrules for his people adverse circumstances and the evil intent of men. Thus God brings to fulfillment his purpose.

God is still in the business of opening ways where we see none. He does this for us as individuals and as members of the community of believers. Like Israel of old we are often commanded to go forward, only to realize with astonishment that we seem to be at the end of the road. Before us there looms only a precipice or a sea. But with God the imperative is the indicative. He never issues a command without giving us the means for completing it. As we move forward in obedience to him, a way is opened up for us. We can then sing with new understanding, "He leadeth me! O blessed tho't!"

Israel's crossing of the sea and her safe passage through the desert speak to us of God's love and of his power. This is fittingly summed up in verse 13, " 'Thou hast led in thy steadfast love the people whom thou hast redeemed, thou has guided them by thy strength to thy holy abode.' " Here God's steadfast love and his strength are brought together as complementary terms.

All of our questions about God could be reduced to only two. They are: "Is he able?" and "Does he care?" To believe in a God who was concerned about our predicament but powerless to act would give us no comfort. On the other hand, to believe in a God who was all powerful yet unconcerned about our predicament would leave us as hopeless wanderers in a hostile universe.

True hope is grounded in God's love *and* his power. "Is he able?" "Does he care?" are questions to which Exodus answers with a resounding, Yes! He does not abandon his people beside the sea. Nor does he lose them in the desert. Instead, in his steadfast love and by his strength he leads them all the way to his holy abode (v. 13).

Those of us who look back on Calvary have even more reason to believe in the love and power of God. Why should we ever doubt that God is love when he gave his Son on Calvary? And why should we doubt his power when he raised him from the dead? God does care! He is able! "What then shall we say to this? If God is for us, who is against us? He who did not spare his own Son but gave him up for us all, will he not also give us all things with him?" (Rom. 8:31-32).

One of the most fitting services we render God is worship and praise of
him. Truly man's chief end is to praise God and to enjoy him forever.
One of God's goals in leading Israel out of Egypt was that he might
plant them upon the mountain of his sanctuary (Ex. 15:17). Israel's
destiny was to become a worshiping community, thus being a witness
to the true God before the nations (Ex. 19:6). On Mount Zion she
could continually offer the service of praise to the God who lives and
reigns forever and ever.

From beginning to end the Bible is a book of singing. The morning
stars, we are told, sang the Creator's praise at creation's dawn (Job
38:7). Israel sang the song of redemption at the Red Sea (Ex. 15:1-18).
The angels sang at the Savior's birth (Luke 2:14). And reference has already been made to the final gathering of the redeemed of all ages.
They will assemble beside the sea of glass mingled with fire and sing the
song of Moses and the song of the Lamb, saying, " 'Great and wonderful are thy deeds, O Lord God the Almighty! Just and true are thy ways,
O King of the ages! Who shall not fear and glorify thy name, O Lord?
For thou alone art holy. All nations shall come and worship thee, for
thy judgments have been revealed' " (Rev. 15:3-4).

---

[1]Walter Harrelson, *Interpreting the Old Testament* (New York: Holt, Rinehart and
Winston, Inc., 1964), p. 86.
[2]Clements, *op. cit.,* p. 85.
[3]Childs, *op. cit.,* p. 238.
[4]James Plastaras, *The God of Exodus* (Milwaukee: The Bruce Publishing Company,
1966), p. 193.
[5]From *A Covenant Community* by Daniel D. Rhodes. © M.E. Bratcher 1964. Used by
permission of John Knox Press.
[6]Norbert Lohfink, *The Christian Meaning of the Old Testament,* trans. R.A. Wilson
(Milwaukee: The Bruce Publishing Company, 1968), pp. 79-80.
[7]Joseph H. Gilmore, "He Leadeth Me! O Blessed Thought!" in *Baptist Hymnal,* ed.
William J. Reynolds (Nashville: Convention Press, 1975), p. 218.

Personal Learning Activities

1. Arrange in chronological order, beginning with 1, the following places in Israel's flight from Egypt:
   ____ Etham   ____ Wilderness of Shur   ____ Red Sea
   ____ Succoth   ____ Pi-ha-hiroth
2. The "holy war" motif in the Old Testament has six elements. From the list below select the six:
   ____ (1) The people of God are threatened by superior forces.
   ____ (2) They are reassured that God can deliver.
   ____ (3) They are commanded to go forward.
   ____ (4) They are fearful and hang back.
   ____ (5) They are saved by the Lord's intervention.
   ____ (6) The enemy is terrified and laid prostrate.
   ____ (7) The people of God are careful to give praise to the Lord for the victory.
3. God delivers his people, not around but _____ trouble. (Supply word.)
4. God's deliverance of Israel combined the _____ and the _____ . (Select proper combination from list below.)
   ____ (1) Bizarre, unexpected.
   ____ (2) Plain, ordinary.
   ____ (3) Natural, supernatural.
5. Think about times of God's deliverance through trouble in your own life. How did he do it?
6. Israel's experience of God's deliverance gave rise to faith. Have the events you recalled in response to item 5 done the same in your life?

Answers:

1. 2, 1, 5, 3, 4; 2. (1), (2), (3), (5), (6), (7); 3. *through*; 4. (3); 5. Your answer; 6. Your answer.

6

Pilgrimage in the Wilderness
Exodus 15:22 to 18:27

This section of the book of Exodus tells about the Israelites' journey from the Red Sea to Sinai. It begins with a cycle of three stories having to do with food and drink (15:22-27; 16:1-36; 17:1-7). Besides the food and drink stories, there are two others. The first has to do with an attack upon the Israelites by the Amalekites (17:8-16). The second gives an account of Jethro's visit to the camp of the Israelites (18:1-27).

1. Tested in the Wilderness

In her journey through the wilderness, Israel witnessed many signs of God's special providence. These signs included the sweetening of the water at Marah, the giving of manna, the providential arrival of a flock of quail, and the bringing forth of water from a rock. Unfortunately, each of these gracious acts was preceded by murmuring and rebellion against the Lord. The period of wilderness wandering was a time of testing for Israel.

In a previous chapter of our study we saw how Pharaoh hardened his heart against the Lord. The Bible accused Israel of having done the very same thing once she had arrived in the wilderness. Psalm 95:7-9 reads: "O that today you would hearken to his voice! Harden not your hearts, as at Meribah, as on the day at Massah in the wilderness, when your fathers tested me and put me to the proof, though they had seen my work." The New Testament cites these words in order to exhort Christians not to harden their hearts in unbelief (Heb. 3:7 to 4:10).

The appalling thing about Israel's rebellion in the wilderness was that it came right after her experience at the Red Sea. There she had witnessed a miracle of deliverance. God had shown his mighty power to save even in the face of overwhelming odds. This great event, more than any other, had confirmed Israel's faith in Moses and in the Lord (see Ex. 14:30-31).

And yet in spite of the fact that God had conquered Pharaoh's army, the Israelites seemed to doubt that he could supply their everyday needs of food, water, and protection. Instead of relying upon him in simple trust, they pouted and whined and longed for the fleshpots of Egypt (16:2-3). Later on, faced with a lack of water, they became so hostile toward Moses that he feared for his life (17:3-4).

Moses had almost as much trouble with the Israelites in the wilderness as he had had with Pharaoh in Egypt. A later writer (Ps. 78:40-43) summed up the wilderness experience of Israel in these words:

> How often they rebelled against
>   him in the wilderness
>   and grieved him in the desert!
> They tested him again and again,
>   and provoked the Holy One of
>   Israel.
> They did not keep in mind his
>   power,
>   or the day when he redeemed
>   them from the foe;
> when he wrought his signs in
>   Egypt,
>   and his miracles in the fields of
>   Zoan.

The Israelites were not prepared to pay the price of freedom. They had been enslaved so long that they had become infected with a slave psychology. Slavery is dehumanizing, and its victims soon lose the will to resist. The desert proved too great a test for the feeble faith of the Israelites. They responded to its hardships by longing for the security they had left behind. They forgot their years of servitude and began to glamorize the past. They remembered Egypt as a land of plenty where they ate fish for nothing, not to speak of cucumbers, melons, leeks, onions, and garlic (Num. 11:5). How could they be sure of survival away from the life-giving waters of the Nile?

Rhodes has given a penetrating analysis of the Israelites' preoccupation with the question of survival:

Even if there is a flush of enthusiasm on the part of these refugees, their ardor cools quickly when they have to face up to the problems of survival in a relatively barren wilderness. The difficulties of Egyptian slavery with its attendant bitterness pale in memory as the problems of desert survival mount. They have escaped the taskmaster, to be sure; but in retrospect this taskmaster rapidly becomes identified with security. The wilderness assumes the gigantic proportions of a new taskmaster who offers no security at all. The immediate question is: Can we survive?[1]

A modern Jewish author has written a further word about the slave mentality of the Israelites:

The bread of freedom is a hard bread. The contrast between bread and matzo [that is, unleavened bread] possibly points [up] the contrast between the lush Nile civilization that the Jews left behind them on the first Passover and the gray rubbled desert in which they came into their identity. The Bible tells how they complained to Moses that they could not forget the meat, the cucumbers, the onions that their taskmasters had fed them on the ramparts of Rameses. The whiplash from time to time had been unpleasant, of course. But that memory had faded rapidly as the scars healed in the dry desert air. The memory of the lost security remained.
. . . The generation of Jews that Moses led into the desert collapsed into despair and panic over and over in moments of crisis. Broken by slavery, they could not shake free of improvidence, cowardice, and idol-worship. All the men who had been slaves in Egypt had to die in the desert, and a new generation had to take up their arms and their religion, before the Jews could cross the Jordan.[2]

God's matchless grace shines through in all its splendor in these chapters. He came to the relief of the Israelites time and time again, even as they murmured and complained against him. He sweetened the bitter waters of Marah (Ex. 15:22-25). He spread a table in the desert and supplied it with bread from heaven (Ex. 16; Num. 11:4-35). At Massah (or Meribah) he brought forth water from the rock (Ex. 17:1-7; Num. 20:1-13). God's response to a faithless, complaining people was one of love and compassion.

2. The Peril of Bitter Water *(15:22-26)*

The Israelites faced a series of perils in the wilderness between the Red Sea and Sinai. These included the peril of bitter water, the peril of starvation, the peril of thirst, the peril of enemies, and the peril of poor organization.

After leaving the Red Sea the Israelites entered the wilderness of Shur. Shur is mentioned in several other Old Testament passages (Gen. 16:7; 20:1; 25:18; 1 Sam. 15:7; 27:8). The word itself means "wall." This has led some interpreters to believe that it designated a line of frontier fortresses built on the eastern border of Egypt to keep out invaders. Others think that it was applied to a range of white cliffs parallel to the Mediterranean coast about twelve miles east of the Gulf of Suez. The evidence is insufficient for the exact location to be fixed.

The Israelites reached a spot named Marah. Marah means "bitterness." It had been so named because of the bitter water found there. Upon tasting the water, the people murmured against Moses, saying, "What shall we drink?" (15:24; see Matt. 6:31-33).

Moses' greatness is revealed in his response to the complaint of the people. He responded by taking the matter to the Lord in prayer. The Lord then showed him how to sweeten the bitter water by throwing a certain kind of tree, or shrub, into the water (see 2 Kings 2:19-22).

Verse 25 indicates that through this experience Israel was being tested by God. The root of the verb "to prove" is *nasah,* from which also is derived the name Massah (17:7). Israel was tested and found wanting.

Plastaras has drawn an analogy between the testing of Israel in the wilderness and the later testing of Jesus in similar surroundings:

> Just as in the first exodus, God had named Israel as his firstborn son (Ex. 4:22) and then led Israel into the desert where he was to test them, so also at the moment of the baptism, God called Jesus his "Beloved Son," and then through the Spirit, led him into the wilderness, where Jesus was to be tested. The temptation narrative of

Matthew 4:1-11 can only be understood against the background of the Old Testament wilderness theme. Israel had failed the test in the wilderness. But now Jesus, who is the New Israel, will return to the wilderness to face the very same temptations. Where the first Israel failed, he will be victorious.[3]

The experience at Marah furnished the occasion for the Lord to declare that he was the healer of his people (Ex. 15:25-26; see Num. 21:4-9; Deut. 7:15; Ps. 103:3). He would become the Great Physician to those who obeyed his voice and gave heed to his commands.

3. The Peril of Starvation *(15:27 to 16:36)*

This is the second in the cycle of food and drink stories. Once again the Israelites were in despair. They had escaped from the Egyptians only to fall prey to an inhospitable desert. How could they escape from this desert enemy? The Lord's response was swift and adequate. He rained bread from heaven in the morning and gave them flesh to eat in the evening (16:11-12). For forty years the Israelites ate their food from his table (16:35).

From Marah the Israelites came to Elim (15:27). Elim is a plural form meaning terebinths, or oaks. Settlements were often made near such trees (see Gen. 12:6). Elim has been identified with Wadi Gharandel, a fertile oasis about sixty miles southeast of the modern city of Suez. The Israelites found twelve springs of water and seventy palm trees at Elim. Later Jewish tradition saw a correspondence between these numbers and the twelve tribes and seventy elders of Israel (Num. 11:16).

The chronology of Exodus 16:1 indicates that about a month had passed since the Israelites had left Egypt (see Ex. 12:6). This was long enough for them to use up all the provisions they had brought with them. They suddenly faced the possibility of starvation.

Hunger is a degrading force. Take away a man's food and he grows dull and listless. He becomes a master of the art of avoiding responsibility and expending little energy. We may not excuse the Jews, but we can at least understand why they reacted to hunger as they did.

Faced with the possibility of starvation, they cried out against Moses and Aaron, " 'Would that we had died by the hand of the Lord in the land of Egypt, when we sat by the fleshpots and ate bread to the full; for you have brought us out into this wilderness to kill this whole assembly with hunger' " (16:3).

The Lord responded to this outcry without waiting for Moses to intercede. He promised that he would rain bread from heaven for the people (v. 4). Again it is stated that through this experience Israel was being tested, to see " 'whether they will walk in my law or not.' " And so the bread from heaven was sent not only to satisfy the hunger of the people but also to teach them to rely entirely upon God's providence. They were told to gather a day's portion every day, except on the sixth day, when they were to gather enough for the sabbath also. God provided just as much as each person needed for his daily ration, but no more. In this way the Israelites were taught to trust God entirely for their daily bread. Jesus taught his followers to have a like faith (see Matt. 6:11). The didactic purpose behind the giving of the bread from heaven is further explained in Deuteronomy 8:3, " 'He humbled you and let you hunger and fed you with manna, which you did not know, nor did your fathers know; that he might make you know that man does not live by bread alone, but that man lives by everything that proceeds out of the mouth of the Lord.' "

When the Christian reads of the bread sent from heaven, he may think of the words of Jesus as recorded in John 6:48-51: " 'I am the bread of life. Your fathers ate the manna in the wilderness, and they died. This is the bread which comes down from heaven, that a man may eat of it and not die. I am the living bread which came down from heaven; if anyone eats of this bread, he will live for ever.' "

Exodus 16:7 contains the promise of Moses and Aaron to the children of Israel that they would see the glory of the Lord. The fulfillment of this promise is recorded in 16:10. The Hebrew word for glory is *kabod*. Its root meaning is "to be heavy." Glory is that which indicates the weight, honor, or dignity of an individual. When used of God, it refers to the revelation of his power and holiness. The glory usually appears in the Old Testament as a bright light or a burning fire enveloped in a cloud. The cloud is there to protect the eyes of the beholder from the glory's blinding brightness. The glory therefore both conceals and reveals God. It reveals enough to confirm men's faith and conceals enough to stimulate their reverence and quicken their devotion.

Verses 12 and 13 speak as if the giving of the quail preceded the giving of the manna. However, according to a later account (Num. 11:4-9,31-33), the quail were sent only after the people complained of the monotony of the diet of manna. The account in the book of Numbers tells how the quail were brought by a wind from the direction of the Mediterranean Sea and how they covered the ground to a depth of two cubits, or approximately three feet.

The commentaries point out that quail are numerous in the Sinai desert, especially in the spring of the year. They spend the winter in Africa and Arabia and then migrate north in the spring in very large flocks. The time of the Exodus was also in the spring of the year, making it coincide with the migrations of the flocks of quail. Exhausted by their flight over the eastern edge of the Mediterranean Sea, the quail could easily be caught by hand or with nets. The fact that this was an annual occurrence did not keep it from being interpreted as a special sign of God's providence.

The brief reference to the quail (Ex. 16:13) is followed by the much longer account of the giving of the manna and the special provision for observing the sabbath (16:14-36).

The manna fell with the dew at night and could be seen in the morning as "a fine, flake-like thing, fine as hoarfrost on the ground" (v. 14). When the Israelites saw it, they exclaimed, " 'What is it?' " Their question appears in Hebrew as *man hu,* from which is derived, by similarity of sound, the name "manna."

Other characteristics of the manna are given in the Scriptures. According to Exodus 16:16, the amount needed to feed each person per day was an omer, that is, slightly more than two quarts. Verses 17 and 18 report that the people gathered varying amounts, but it all came out to be just enough for each one's needs. Verse 18 was quoted by Paul in 2 Corinthians 8:15 to encourage Christian generosity. The principle laid down by Paul was that each should give according to his ability and each should receive according to his need.

The manna bred worms and stank when kept overnight (16:20). It had to be gathered early in the morning, because "when the sun grew hot, it melted" (16:21). It could be prepared in various ways, including boiling and baking (16:23). "It was like coriander seed, white, and the taste of it was like wafers made with honey" (16:31). Coriander seed were used for seasoning, very much as caraway and sesame seed are used today. All in all, the manna seems to have been a rather monotonous (see Num. 11:4-9). It was edible enough, but the Israelites soon grew tired of it. Compared to what they had been accustomed to in Egypt, it was poor fare indeed.

Many interpreters have supposed that the manna used to feed the Israelites in the desert came from the tamarisk tree. Even today in the Sinai peninsula a substance like honey is produced by scale insects which feed on the sap of the tamarisk. The bedouins gather it in the early morning, boil it, strain it, and use it like honey. Their name for it is *mann.*

While there may be some points of similarity between manna and the modern *mann,* one would have to agree with the conclusions of Hyatt, "There are many features of the manna as described in the biblical passages which do not fit the modern *mann:* the great quantities in which it could be gathered, its automatic adjustment to the needs of each person, its failure to appear on the Sabbath, its being made into cakes, its putrefaction if kept until morning, and its ability to feed the Hebrews over a period of forty years."[4]

According to Exodus 16:35, the Israelites continued to eat manna for forty years, until they reached the border of Canaan. Joshua 5:12 relates that the manna ceased when they reached Gilgal. After that they ate the produce of the land of Canaan.

Exodus 16:32-34 reports that the Lord commanded Moses and Aaron to take a jar, put an omer of manna in it, and place it before the testimony to be kept throughout all their generations. The testimony is another name for the ark of the covenant (see Ex. 30:36). According to Hebrews 9:1-5, the ark of the covenant contained, among other things, a golden urn filled with manna. By preserving the jar of manna, Israel was constantly reminded of how God had preserved her life in the wilderness.

4. The Peril of Thirst *(17:1-7)*

Thirst is no less a threat to survival than hunger. As the Israelites journeyed across the desert, they were often faced with a shortage of water. Each demonstration of God's providence in supplying water was at the same time an occasion of sin and rebellion on the part of Israel. This is clearly not the kind of story a nation would have invented about itself. From beginning to end it glorifies the God of Israel at Israel's expense.

The shortage of water occurred in the wilderness of Sin at a place called Rephidim (Ex. 17:1). The wilderness of Sin lay in the Sinai peninsula near the traditional site of Mount Sinai. It is to be distinguished from the wilderness of Zin (Num. 20:1), a region lying to the southwest of the Dead Sea near Kadesh. Rephidim is usually identified with the Wadi Refayid, which lies in the southern part of the Sinai peninsula.

The story in Exodus 17:1-7 reflects the usual pattern found in the murmuring accounts: a need arises; the people immediately turn upon Moses; Moses intercedes before the Lord for help; and the need is met.

A significant feature of this story is the way in which Moses was told to provide water for the people to drink. He was told to take some of the elders of Israel with him and to go to Horeb, another name for

Sinai (17:6). He was to take in his hand the rod with which Aaron had struck the Nile, turning its waters into blood (Ex. 7:20). The Lord would stand before Moses on the rock at Horeb and Moses was to strike the rock with his rod. This would cause water to come from the rock and the threat of death by thirst would be averted.

The Hebrew word for rock in verse 6 is *tsur*. It normally refers to a rock mass, such as a stone mountain or cliff. The word for a loose rock or a detached stone is *'eben*. Caves were often located in the sides of a *tsur* (see Ex. 33:21,22; Isa. 2:10). A spring might also flow from the side of a *tsur*. However, this does not mean that one should attempt to rationalize the story of how Moses brought water from the rock. Childs' statement is right on target, "The whole point of the story turns on the gracious and surprising provision of God who provided water for his people when none was available."[5]

The place where Moses opened a spring in the rock was called Massah, from the Hebrew verb *nasah,* meaning "put to the proof, test, try." It was also called Meribah, from the verb *rib,* meaning "to find fault, contend." Psalm 95:7-11 is a later commentary on the significance of these two names as designating the place where the Israelites who had come out of Egypt rebelled against the Lord and lost their right to enter the Promised Land. A similar account of water being brought from the rock is found in Numbers 20:2-13. This later account attributes sin to Moses and Aaron also. Because of their sin they too were barred from entering the land of Canaan.

Exodus 17:6 was interpreted by ancient rabbis to mean that the water-producing rock followed the Jews on all their journeys through the wilderness, furnishing them with a constant supply of fresh water.[6] Paul evidently had this tradition in mind when he wrote: "I want you to know, brethren, that our fathers were all under the cloud, and all passed through the sea . . . and all ate the same supernatural food and all drank the same supernatural drink. For they drank from the supernatural Rock which followed them, and the Rock was Christ" (1 Cor. 10:1,3-4).

5. The Peril of Enemies *(17:8-16)*

As the Israelites journeyed toward Sinai, they encountered the Amalekites, who attacked them. This is the first account of armed conflict involving the Israelites after their departure from Egypt. It is not possible to identify the specific locality of the battle.

For the first time in the Exodus account, Joshua appears on the scene. He was the leader of the Israelite forces. From the author's viewpoint, however, it was actually Moses who directed the battle, and its outcome depended on what he did.

The Amalekites were a nomadic tribe living in the desert south of Judah (see Gen. 14:7). According to Genesis 36:12, Amalek was the grandson of Esau. The Amalekites, along with the Canaanites, tried to prevent the Israelites' entering Canaan (Num. 14:43-45). Later both Saul (1 Sam. 15) and David (1 Sam. 30) had to do battle with them. According to 1 Chronicles 4:43, the Amalekites as a people were finally destroyed in the time of Hezekiah. The memory of the hatred between Jews and Amalekites is preserved in the book of Esther. There we learn that Mordecai outwitted Haman the Agagite, a descendant of Agag. Agag, who was slain by Samuel (1 Sam. 15:32-33), was a king of the Amalekites.

At first sight the story of the battle between Israel and the Amalekites seems to suggest that magic was involved. Moses took a position on top of a hill overlooking the valley where the armies were clashing. He then raised his hand. In some mysterious way his raised hand enabled Israel to advance against the enemy. But when he grew weary and lowered his hand, the tide of battle went the other way. Finally, when he was exhausted and could no longer raise his hands, he was seated on a stone and his hands were supported on either side by Aaron and Hur. In this way the Israelites emerged the victors.

Nothing in the story suggests that Moses had his hand raised in prayer. No words of prayer are recorded. Rather, the raising of his hand seems to have been a form of prophetic symbolism, a symbolic gesture indicating that the Lord had delivered the Amalekites into the hands of Israel. Often in the Old Testament hands are the means of mediating power (see Isa. 9:12,17,21). People of Old Testament times believed that a symbolic action, such as raising the hand against an enemy, carried with it the power of its own fulfillment.

With the help of Moses on the mountain, Joshua gained an impressive victory in the valley. Verse 13 says that he "mowed down Amalek and his people with the edge of the sword." After the battle had ended, the Israelites raised a victory altar and named it "The Lord is my banner" (vv. 15-16). "Banner" (Hebrew: *nes*) is a relatively rare word in the Old Testament and occurs only twenty-one times. The meaning seems to be that Moses with his hand raised toward heaven served as a banner or standard, rallying the people of Israel and inspiring them to fight under the Lord their king.

The Lord charged Moses to write down Israel's victory over the Amalekites as a memorial in a book (v. 14). This may be a reference to the book of Jashar, a book no longer extant, but quoted from time to time in the Old Testament (see Josh. 10:13; 2 Sam. 1:18). Or the reference may be to another lost book, the Book of the Wars of the Lord (see Num. 21:14).

Moses bitterly resented the attack upon Israel by the Amalekites. He proclaimed that the Lord himself would fight against Amalek from generation to generation and that he would utterly blot out the remembrance of Amalek from under the sun. The purpose of this story in Exodus is to show how the Lord saved his pilgrim people from every threat. This story, unlike the others, makes no reference to murmuring on the part of Israel.

6. The Peril of Poor Organization *(18:1-27)*

Jethro's visit to the camp of the Israelites is a delightful interlude in the sequence of otherwise stormy events that make up the Exodus. By the time the reader reaches this point in the story, he is likely to be emotionally exhausted. He has read about plagues, death at midnight, danger by the sea, and perils in the wilderness. But now the writer pauses for a moment to reminisce and to rejoice. The whole story breathes an air of oriental graciousness that warms the heart. Perhaps one of the reasons the writer placed the material at this particular point was to draw a contrast between the good which Jethro did for Israel and the harm which Amalek had inflicted upon her.

Jethro, Moses' father-in-law, appeared at the mountain of God where the Israelites were encamped (v. 5). He brought with him Moses' wife, Zipporah (meaning "Lady Bird"), and Moses' two sons, Gershom and Eliezer (see Acts 7:29). This is the first reference to Zipporah after the strange story of the circumcision of her son in Exodus 4:24-26. According to 18:2, Moses had sent his wife and their two sons back from Egypt to Midian, possibly for safekeeping. Jewish tradition reports that when Aaron first met Moses (Ex. 4:27), Aaron persuaded his younger brother to send his family back to Midian in order not to add to the number of unfortunates in Egypt.

The meeting between Moses and Jethro resulted in a spontaneous outburst of family affection. Although Moses did not kiss his wife in public—this would have been highly improper—he and his father-in-law kissed each other in true oriental style.

After the two men had asked about each other's welfare, Moses invited Jethro to his tent (18:7). There he related to him all that the Lord had done for Israel from the time of their sojourn in Egypt until they had reached this spot. He simply bore witness to the greatness and goodness of the Lord. The scene is unforgettable—Moses seated in his desert tent, recounting the mighty acts of God to his Midianite father-in-law. What would happen if we should begin to bear witness to our faith with the same simplicity and the same enthusiasm?

Jethro's reaction to Moses' speech was threefold; he acknowledged the greatness of Israel's God through praise, through confession, and through sacrifice. First, he blessed the Lord (v. 10). To bless God means more than to praise him. It means to acknowledge with thanksgiving that one's trust in his care and guidance has been fully vindicated (see Gen. 24:27; Ruth 4:14; 1 Kings 1:48). Second, Jethro offered a confession (v. 11). His confession begins with the emphatic statement, " 'Now I know.' " These words are used in the Scriptures to express a conviction arrived at through observation and experience (see Gen. 22:12; 1 Kings 17:24; 2 Kings 5:15). Jethro's confession was that he now knew that Israel's God was greater than all other gods, since he had rescued his people from Egypt. Some have interpreted this as Jethro's conversion to faith in the God of Israel and renunciation of his own pagan past. At the very least, Jethro acknowledged the power of Israel's God as witnessed to by Moses. Third, Jethro's final act of worship was to offer a burnt offering and sacrifices to God (v. 12). Aaron and the elders of Israel partook of his sacrifices in what was obviously a covenant meal. One is impressed by the absence of any spirit of sectarianism in this passage. The Israelites did not hesitate to share in a sacrificial feast with Jethro, even though he was a priest of Midian (18:1; see Gen. 14:18-20). Jethro was not treated as an outsider, but was welcomed as a brother.

Jethro spent the following day watching Moses as he sat judging the people (v. 13). Verse 16 informs us that Moses did not rely on his own wisdom alone in fulfilling this responsibility, but made known to the people "the statutes of God and his decisions." In this capacity he served as mediator between the people and God. He handed on to them the divine teaching related to the resolving of their differences. Already in this passage there is a foreshadowing of Moses' role as lawgiver to Israel.

When Jethro saw that the burden of responsibility was too great for Moses alone, he offered him some fatherly advice. He counseled him to share his responsibility with others, lest he exhaust himself and the people by trying to carry the burden alone. Moses would still be expected to handle the harder cases, but his subordinates would handle the more routine work. This would result in a better use of resources and personnel. It was a wise solution to the problem of poor organization.

Jethro mentioned four qualifications that Moses must look for in the men appointed to share his responsibility (v. 21): (1) They had to be men who were qualified for the job—" 'able men' "; (2) they had to be God-fearing men—" 'such as fear God' "; (3) they had to be men of truth, whose word could be accepted at face value—" 'men who are trustworthy' "; (4) they had to be men who could not be corrupted by money—" 'men who hate a bribe.' " These qualifications were to be applied all across the board, whether a man was being appointed ruler of thousands, of hundreds, of fifties, or of tens. The same high standards were demanded of all public officials selected to serve under Moses.

This is perhaps the finest list of qualifications for public officials to be found anywhere in the Scriptures. How different the government in our own country would be if our leaders were chosen according to these standards!

Moses took the advice of Jethro, and the story ends on a happy note. Jethro had accomplished a good purpose through his visit, and he presently left to return to his own land. He did not accompany the Israelites to Canaan, although some of his children did (Judg. 1:16).

Fleming James has summarized what this story teaches about Moses in the following words:

> The story illustrates three traits of Moses: his devotion to the people, his readiness to take advice, and his willingness to delegate authority. The conscientious judge who sits for hours listening to disputes which have no personal concern for him is in all cultures an example of unselfish dedication to the public good. He who takes criticism constructively will be ever learning new and better methods. And he who knows how to turn over to others work which is within their powers will build up an organization of loyal helpers and multiply his effectiveness many fold. Such a leader was Moses.[7]

7. Lessons for Life from the Scriptures
Israel's experiences in the wilderness should teach us that following God often means being willing to sacrifice present security for a higher goal. Someone has characterized Americans who live in the second half of the twentieth century as a hothouse-bred generation, willing to settle for easy success rather than risk great failure. Christian character is not developed in a hothouse environment. God tests them whom he calls, not in order to reject them, but that their dross may be consumed and their gold refined.

Rhodes poses some questions for us to ponder before we too easily pass judgment on the Israelites:

> If you had been a Hebrew in Goshen, would you have
> been ready to make a dash for freedom? If you had been
> a Hungarian in 1956, would you have joined the
> Hungarian revolt? If you had been a parent with young
> children in either of these situations, how would this
> have affected your attitude and actions? In advising your
> children about vocational possibilities, what weight do
> you give to considerations of material and physical
> security? What factors would you rate as more important
> than these? If your child showed any interest in becom-
> ing a missionary to one of the turbulent new nations,
> would you encourage or discourage him? On what
> basis?[8]

*In spite of the fact that God had wrought a marvelous deliverance at the
Red Sea, Israel found dependence upon God to supply her daily needs of
food, drink, and protection difficult.* She was constantly whining and
complaining, and asking "What shall we eat?" "What shall we drink?"
"Who will take care of us?"

Is this an apt description of the attitude that we often assume?
Though we have trusted God to save us from sin and death, we often
fail to trust him for our daily bread. When irritations and inconve-
niences arise, we often fret and complain just as Israel did.

We have seen demonstrations of divine grace far greater than anything that happened in Israel in the Exodus. We live in memory of the
redemption from past bondage and in anticipation of the promised inheritance at the end of our pilgrimage. We too find ourselves in the
wilderness, somewhere between the Red Sea and the Promised Land.
And how difficult it is for us to follow God in simple trust!

These stories should warn us against the sins of ingratitude and unbelief.
(See Pss. 95:7-11; 78:11-43; 105:26-45; 106:6-33.) Israel's wilderness
experience illustrates both the innate tendency of Israel to disbelieve
God and God's readiness to provide for her in spite of her unbelief.

From this experience we can learn the meaning not only of faith but
also of faithlessness. Faithlessness is the unwillingness to trust God
when there is no other sign of hope. Sin springs from this, for it is the
very nature of sin that it is born of doubt and nurtured by anxiety.
Faith, on the other hand, is letting the reins of one's life fall into the
hands of God. It is trusting him completely, even in the face of circum-

stances that belie such a trust (see Dan. 3:16-18). God give us such a faith!

―――
[1]Rhodes, *op. cit.* pp. 32-33.
[2]Herman Wouk, *This Is My God* (Garden City: Doubleday & Company, Inc., 1959), pp. 72-73.
[3]Plastaras, *op. cit.,* pp. 284-85.
[4]Hyatt, *op. cit.,* p. 177.
[5]Childs, *op. cit.,* p. 308.
[6]Cohen, *op. cit.,* p. 431.
[7]James, *op. cit.,* pp. 25-26.
[8]Rhodes, *op. cit.,* p. 32.

Personal Learning Activities

1. Signs of God's special providence for Israel in the wilderness wanderings included (select correct responses):
   ___ (1) Sweetening of water at Marah (Ex. 15:22-25).
   ___ (2) Provision of manna (Ex. 16:13-16).
   ___ (3) Provision of quail (Ex. 16:13).
   ___ (4) Water from rock at Massah (Ex. 17:1-7).
2. Preceding God's provision each time, the children of Israel responded to their situation with (select one):
   ___ (1) Prayer.   ___ (3) Murmuring.
   ___ (2) Praise.   ___ (4) Joy at deliverance from
                                              Egypt.
3. My response to hard times is _____ similar, _____ dissimilar to Israel's.
4. The wilderness wanderings were a time of testing for Israel. Similarly, hardship can be a time of our testing. What have you learned about yourself and God in such times? Have you learned to trust God?
5. Moses is an example to Christian leaders in at least three ways. From the list below select the correct responses:
   ___ (1) He got angry when tired.
   ___ (2) He was devoted to his people.
   ___ (3) He listened carefully to wise counsel.
   ___ (4) He delegated authority.
6. Review your selections above, and test yourself as a Christian leader by Moses' exemplary traits.

———

Answers:

1. All responses; 2. (3); 3. Your answer; 4. Your answer; 5. (2), (3), (4); 6. Your answer.

7

Covenant and Commitment

Exodus 19:1-25; 20:18-21; 24:1-18;

31:18 to 32:35;

34:1-35

A milestone was reached when the Israelites arrived at Mount Sinai. This destination had been their immediate goal from the moment they set out from Egypt. It was at this mountain that God had appeared to Moses in the burning bush and had sent him on his mission. At that time Moses had requested proof of the reality of his call. God had assured him that he finally would know that he had been divinely called and commissioned when he had freed the Israelites from bondage and had brought them to this mountain to serve God (see Ex. 3:12). At last the moment of proof had come!

As the Israelites stood before the mountain of God, their minds must have been filled with memories of the recent past. They recalled how they had been liberated from Egypt, how they had escaped the forces of Pharaoh at the sea, and how they had overcome the perils of the desert. Now at last they stood before the rugged peaks of Mount Sinai, at the very spot where God had first appeared to Moses. They had an appointment to keep with God. Before they could go on their way to claim the land he had promised to their fathers, their relationship to him had to be sealed in a covenant.

Most modern authorities identify the mountain of the covenant with Jebul Musa, meaning in Arabic "Mountain of Moses." Jebul Musa lies fifty-five miles north of the southernmost tip of the Sinai peninsula. It reaches a height of 7,467 feet above sea level and rises 2,600 feet above the surrounding plateau. It can be scaled in approximately one and one-half hours.

A modern archaeologist has described the approach to Mount Sinai in these terms:

> The multicolored granite hills sparkle in the bright sun and the occasional scrub brush serves to reinforce the starkness. And it is quiet. Little lives in this place, and the stillness is extraordinary. Suddenly the seemingly endless ravines give way to a plain beyond which an awe-inspiring mountain of red granite rises 2,600 feet above the plateau. This is Sinai.[1]

According to Exodus 19:1, the Israelites arrived at Sinai about three months after they had left Egypt. Numbers 10:11-12 places their departure from Sinai in the second month of the second year of their pilgrimage. This means that their stay at Sinai lasted almost a year. During this time three tremendously significant events took place: (1) God appeared as he had appeared to Moses earlier (Ex. 3:1-6), and his self-revelation was accompanied by mighty convulsions in the realm of nature; (2) a covenant was established between him and his people; (3) the law was given to guide the people in their covenant obligations.

It is well for us to recall the point we have reached in our study of the book of Exodus. The basic themes of the book are four: (1) the oppression of the Israelites and their deliverance from Egypt (Ex. 1—15); (2) guidance in the wilderness (Ex. 16—18); (3) covenant-making at Sinai (Ex. 19—24; 32—34); and (4) the building of the tabernacle and its furnishings, and the organization of worship (Ex. 25—31; 35—40). This chapter is concerned mainly with covenant-making at Sinai.

1. The Old Testament Concept of Covenant

Before we turn to the text of Scripture, it would help us to review the Old Testament concept of covenant. Many interpreters view the covenant concept as the cord that binds the various parts of the Old Testament together. Much recent study in the theology of the Old Testament has affirmed the centrality of the covenant to an understanding of Israel's relationship to God.

The Hebrew word for covenant is *berith*. It appears no less than 286 times in the Hebrew text of the Old Testament. Its basic meaning is "bond" or "fetter." A covenant was a contract or treaty binding two parties together.

Covenants could be made between individuals, as in the case of David and Jonathan (1 Sam. 18:1-4). Or they could be made between tribes or nations, as in the case of the Israelites and the Gibeonites (Josh. 9:3-27).

The term most commonly used in the Old Testament for making a covenant is "cutting a covenant." The term apparently arose from the custom of slaying a sacrificial animal, cutting it into pieces, arranging the pieces in two parallel rows, and requiring those entering into the covenant to pass between the two rows (see Gen. 15:9-21; Jer. 34:18-20). This arrangement seems to have been symbolic; if either party should break the covenant or fail to fulfill its obligations, he would suffer a fate similar to that of the sacrificial animal.

There are two basic kinds of covenants in the Old Testament. The first kind involved covenants made between equals. These are often referred to as parity covenants. The covenant between David and Jonathan fell within this category. Such covenants imposed mutual obligations on both parties.

The second kind involved covenants between unequals, as between a king and his subjects, or vassals. These are referred to as vassal or suzerainty (ruler) covenants. Such a covenant did not bind the two parties together as equals.

The covenant between God and Israel was of this latter type. God and Israel were not bound together as equals. Rather, the Sinai covenant was a covenant offered by the stronger to the weaker. It was offered to Israel as an undeserved blessing and honor. God had already redeemed her and led her out of bondage. Through the covenant he now offered her the privilege of coming under his rule and living in obedience to the laws of his realm. Once Israel accepted the covenant and its terms, she was bound to carry it out. To fail in that was to forfeit the covenant's promise.

Those persons who entered into a covenant bound themselves by solemn oath to be loyal and faithful and to assist and support one another whenever the need arose. The Old Testament had a special word for the personal commitment expected of a covenant partner. It was the word *hesed,* a word which cannot be translated adequately by any single word in English. It combines the ideas of love, loyalty, and ready response to need. It has been variously rendered as "mercy," "grace," "love," "loving-kindness," "steadfast love," and "loyal love." It is by all standards one of the richest words in the Hebrew vocabulary.

The Old Testament reports three major covenants made between God and his people. The first covenant was made with Noah (Gen. 6:18; 9:8-17). The second was made between God and Abraham (Gen.

15; 17:1-14). However, the covenant made between God and Israel at Sinai involved all Israel, and was therefore the most significant. It is to this covenant that we now turn our attention.

2. God's Invitation and Israel's Response *(19:1-9)*

Six steps in covenant-making are highlighted in Exodus 19—24. They are: (1) the invitation to the people to enter into the covenant relationship, and their ready response (19:1-9); (2) the preparations of the people prior to the third day (19:10-15); (3) the appearance of God on the third day (19:16-25); (4) the proclamation of the Ten Commandments, the basic law of the covenant (20:1-17); (5) the appointment of Moses as mediator (20:18-21); and (6) the sealing of the covenant (24:1-18).

Israel's arrival and encampment at Sinai occurred three months after her departure from Egypt (19:1-2). Once the Israelites had arrived at Sinai, Moses left them and went up the mountain to meet God (19:3). There the Lord called to him and gave him a message to take back to the congregation waiting at the foot of the mountain (19:4-6).

The message given to Moses is found in verses 4-6. The message began by reminding Israel of what the Lord had already done for her. It told of his power to save, as demonstrated in the Exodus out of Egypt. But it told more. It told how the Lord bore these people as on the wings of eagles and brought them to himself. Israel was safely transported across the desert, as an eagle bears its young (see Deut. 32:10-12). The reference to the rescue of the people as "on eagles' wings" emphasized the swiftness, the security, and the affectionate care with which the deliverance from Egypt had been accomplished. Significant also is the statement that God brought Israel to himself. The ultimate goal of those who left Egypt was more than reaching a distant mountain or even a distant Promised Land. The ultimate goal was to encounter the living God and to enter into a new covenant relationship with him.

The second part of the message had to do with Israel's obligation under the covenant, with her character and mission as the people of the covenant. On the basis of past favors bestowed, God offered to establish a unique relationship with Israel.

God's offer was prefaced by the words, " 'Now therefore, if . . .' " (19:5). Israel's entry into the covenant had to be of her own free choice. However, if she chose to enter the covenant, it had to be in accord with conditions laid down by God. She had to be willing to obey his voice and keep his covenant. It was he who set the standards for admission and not she. The Hebrew word "to obey" also means "to hear." Old Testament writers believed that a person had not truly heard God unless he also obeyed him. Is that not an accurate concept?

If Israel were obedient and kept the covenant, she would enter into a unique relationship with God. Three phrases are used to spell out this uniqueness: " 'my own possession' " (v. 5); " 'a kingdom of priests' " (v. 6); " 'a holy nation' " (v. 6). We will examine each of these in detail.

God commanded Moses to say to Israel, " 'You shall be my own possession among all peoples; for all the earth is mine' " (v. 5). *The New English Bible* translates "my own possession" "my special possession." Behind this phrase there is only one Hebrew word, the word *segullah*. It is a relatively rare word, being used only eight times in the entire Old Testament. Of these uses, two refer to the private treasure of a king (1 Chron. 29:3; Eccl. 2:8), and six refer symbolically to Israel as God's special treasure or possession (Ex. 19:5; Deut. 7:6; 14:2; 26:18; Ps. 135:4; Mal. 3:17). This term passed over into the New Testament by way of the Septuagint and came to be used to represent the Christian's unique relationship to God through Christ (Eph. 1:14; 2 Thess. 2:14; Titus 2:14; 1 Pet. 2:9).

G.A.F. Knight has beautifully described the significance of this unusual word:

> In olden days a king was the ultimate owner of every-thing in the land he ruled. He owned every building, ev-ery farm, every coin. But that kind of 'owning' could give him little personal satisfaction. Consequently in his palace he kept a treasure chest of his 'very own', in which he delighted to store the precious stones and *objets d'art* which he loved to handle. This treasure chest was his *segullah*. In the same way, God, who made the whole earth, and to whom all nations belonged, looked now upon Israel as his own peculiar treasure.[2]

It is important to note that God's offer to make Israel his own special possession did not mean that he had surrendered his claim on other nations. In fact, the statement concerning Israel's special relationship to him is followed immediately by "for all the earth is mine." No, God had not given up on the nations. Rather, he was calling Israel to be his special possession *because* all the earth was his. There was a universal purpose in his calling of Israel, the same purpose stated earlier in the calling of Abraham (Gen. 12:1-3). It was that through her all the nations of the earth might be blessed. Israel was to be the pilot project in God's plan to redeem all nations. In choosing her, God was establishing a beachhead in human history from which he would never be dislodged until his worldwide purpose had been achieved.

The second phrase used to spell out Israel's unique role under the covenant is "a kingdom of priests" (19:6). This phrase occurs only here in the Old Testament. It has been translated in several different ways by ancient versions and by the New Testament.[3] The Septuagint reads "a royal priesthood." The Vulgate has "a priestly kingdom." The Peshitta[4] translates "a kingdom and priests." The Targums[5] read "kings and priests." In the New Testament, 1 Peter 2:9 reads "a royal priesthood," thus following the Septuagint. Revelation 5:10 reads, "a kingdom and priests," the same reading as that of the Peshitta (see also Rev. 1:6; 20:6).

One way to interpret "a kingdom of priests" is to say that all Israelites were to become priests. As such they would all have the right of direct access to God. They would become mature enough spiritually that they would no longer need intermediaries to bring them into communion with God. The expression has most often been interpreted and applied this way. When Protestants speak of "the priesthood of all believers," this is usually what they mean.

However, an alternate interpretation has been proposed by other scholars. R.B.Y. Scott[6] is representative of this group. Scott believes Exodus 19:6 designates "a kingdom set apart like a priesthood," one possessing collectively the priestly status of a holy nation. Israel was not to be a nation composed of individuals who were all priests. Rather, Israel herself was to be a priest-nation. What the Levitical priests were within Israel, Israel was to be among the nations. Israel's privilege was great, but her responsibility was greater still. She was to exercise a priestly role on behalf of all nations, making intercession for them and instructing them in the ways of God. Ultimately, according to Scott's interpretation, the primary emphasis in this verse is upon missionary outreach.

The third phrase employed in verse 6, "a holy nation," teaches that mission is ultimately rooted and grounded in character. If Israel is to be a kingdom of priests, she must also be a holy nation. Holiness and vocation are inseparable.

The basic meaning of holiness is to be separated or set apart so as to belong to God. For example, a day becomes a holy day when it is set apart from all other days and dedicated to the service of God. A place becomes a holy place whenever it is associated with the self-revelation of God. A person becomes a holy person whenever he is consecrated to God. The main emphasis therefore in the concept of holiness is positive rather than negative. Merely being separated does not cause something to be holy; belonging to God does. Israel was to be devoted to God; she was to be his special heritage. She was to be set apart from the nations (a holy nation) in order that she might minister to the nations (a kingdom of priests). Her privilege was matched only by her responsibility. Her priestly ministry demanded total commitment.

Israel's special vocation was not to be forced on her, but left to her free choice. Therefore when Moses descended the mountain, he called together the elders of the people and set before them the requirements for those entering into a covenant with God (19:7). They had to decide whether or not they wished to proceed further with this matter. Their response was enthusiastically affirmative, "All that the Lord has spoken we will do." It was a covenant freely offered and freely accepted.

3. The Cleansing of Israel *(19:10-15)*

A new section begins with verse 10. It describes the purification of the Israelites and the preparations they made prior to the third day of the covenant-making procedures.

God commanded Moses to have the people consecrate themselves and be ready for the third day, when he would come down upon the mountain. Not only their hearts but even their garments had to be cleansed. The point of this passage is that it is a serious matter for people to approach God. Those who do so must give attention even to their physical appearance.

The Israelites were specifically commanded to spend two days consecrating themselves in preparation for their encounter with the holy God. They were to wash their garments and make sure they kept their distance from the sacred mountain. Only when the trumpet sounded a long blast were they to come near (v. 13). They were also to refrain from sexual contact with a woman (v. 15; see Lev. 15:18).

4. The Appearance of God *(19:16-25)*

This section tells of the final arrival of the third day. This was the long-awaited day, the appointed time of God's appearing on Mount Sinai. It must have been a moment fraught with great emotion. The experience at Sinai was one of the most awesome in all of Hebrew history. The God who had revealed himself as Redeemer now showed himself as the Holy One. He was the one set apart from all others. His very presence evoked fear and wonder.

On the morning of the third day the people came with great expectation to the foot of the mountain to await the appearance of God. The reader senses the feeling of awe and terror that must have gripped them as they watched Moses slowly climbing the mountain to meet God. As he scaled the granite peaks, he was surrounded by thunder, lightning, earthquake, trumpet sound, fire, and smoke. All nature was in commotion at this divine-human encounter. The climax to the whole scene is described in verse 9. When the trumpet sound reached its highest pitch, Moses could be seen speaking to God, while God answered him in thunderclaps. What a conversation that must have been!

The Sinai account pictures God as revealing himself in the more violent aspects of nature (see also 1 Kings 19:9-12; Pss. 18:6-15; 29:1-11). Smoke, clouds, lightning, thunder, fire, and earthquake accompanied his self-revelation. And yet he is far more than a mere nature god. He is the God who rules over nature and through it makes himself known to men (see Ps. 19:1-6). Nature is his creation and must serve his purpose. He is the sovereign Lord of creation and of history.

Verses 20-25 indicate that the preparations for guarding the sacredness of the mountain were still regarded by God as inadequate. It is interesting that Moses disputed the need for further protection. This is in line with Moses' tendency to want to argue with God. The positive value in this is that it helped him to become a great intercessor.

5. Moses' Appointment as Mediator *(20:18-21)*

A major step in the covenant-making process was the giving of the Ten Commandments (20:1-17) and the Book of the Covenant (20:22 to 23:33). We will pass over these bodies of law for the present. They will be examined in detail in the next chapter of this study.

Reference has already been made to the high drama being played out before the eyes of the Israelites as Moses climbed the mountain and engaged in conversation with God. When Moses had reached the summit of the mountain and God began to speak to him in successive crashes of thunder, the people could stand the tension no longer. Suddenly they broke and ran, withdrawing to what they considered a safe distance from the border of the mountain (20:18).

Verse 18 reports that the people were afraid and trembled and stood afar off. The same Hebrew word translated "trembled" occurs in Isaiah 7:2, which reads, "His heart and the heart of his people shook as the trees of the forest shake before the wind." The word sometimes means "to reel," or "to stagger." The stress in verse 18 is upon the terror and utter dismay that seized the Israelites. The vision of God was more than they could stand.

This terrifying experience prompted the people to make a special request of Moses. It was that henceforth he should speak to them for

God, and that God not address them directly (v. 19). This request marks an important watershed in Old Testament religion. It indicates the point when Israel first recognized the need for a mediator between her and God. From this time forward there is no instance in the Old Testament where God speaks directly to the whole congregation of Israel. When he wished to address the nation, he summoned a messenger and gave him the message he wanted delivered. After Moses he raised up prophets, or messengers, like Moses (see Deut. 18:15-19). The way was being prepared for the role of Jesus Christ as Mediator between God and man (see 1 Tim. 2:5).

Seeing their fear and hearing their request, Moses spoke to reassure the people, " 'Do not fear; for God has come to prove you, and that the fear of him may be before your eyes, that you may not sin' " (v. 20). There is a subtle play on the word "fear" in this verse. On the one hand, Moses told the people not to fear. On the other hand, he told them that the constant awareness of the fear of God would keep them from sin. Two different kinds of fear are in focus here. The first is related to anxiety and terror. It is unsuitable for the people of God. The second is the reverential awe that one feels when he contemplates God. This is coupled with a sense of dread of offending him. The Israelites were to maintain this sense of reverence and dread of committing offense whenever they approached God. There must be nothing casual or flippant about our attitude in such circumstances.

6. The Sealing of the Covenant *(24:1-18)*
The covenant-making ceremony was finalized by the events described in chapter 24.

First, preparation was made for Moses, Aaron, Nadab, Abihu, and seventy elders of the people to go to meet the Lord on the mountaintop (vv. 1-2). Nadab and Abihu were sons of Aaron (Ex. 6:23). Seventy was considered an ideal number throughout Old Testament times. The seventy elders acted as representatives of the people, since all Israel could not go up the mountain to see God. The seventy elders are mentioned again in Numbers 11:24, which is a continuation of the present narrative.

Before these representatives of Israel went up the mountain, there was a covenant affirmation ceremony at the foot of the mountain (vv. 3-8). The people pledged their acceptance of the covenant twice, once at the outset (v. 3) and again after Moses had read from the Book of the Covenant (v. 7). At the beginning, the Book of the Covenant probably consisted of the Ten Commandments. Later it was expanded to include other legislation.

As a part of the covenant affirmation ceremony, twelve pillars were set up around an altar (v. 4). The twelve pillars symbolized the participation of the twelve tribes of Israel in the ceremony. Burnt offerings and peace offerings were then made by young men chosen from among the people (v. 5). The indication is that they were laymen and not priests.

The role of Moses on this occasion was that of covenant representative or mediator on behalf of all the people. He took the blood of the sacrifices, divided it, and threw half of it against the altar and half of it on the people (vv. 6,8). The blood of the covenant (see Matt. 26:28; 1 Cor. 11:25), thus distributed, was regarded as having established bonds of union between God and Israel.

The final sealing of the covenant came when Moses, the Aaronic priests, and the seventy elders went up the mountain away from the people (vv. 9-11). There near the top of the mountain they saw the God of Israel (v. 10) and participated in a covenant meal (v. 11). The statement in verse 10 that those who went up the mountain "saw God" is clarified by the further statement that God did not lay his hand on these representatives of the people of Israel (v. 11). The implication is that if he had done so, they would have been struck dead. The general view of the Bible is that a person cannot see God and live (see Ex. 33:20; John 1:18).

The covenant meal of verse 11 was no ordinary meal. It was eaten in the presence of God. By eating this meal the representatives of Israel formally accepted on behalf of the entire community the obligations of the covenant. Israel was now solemnly bound to God. In the future any breach of the commandments of God would also be a breach of covenant. The base had been laid for all of God's future dealings with Israel. It would be impossible to exaggerate the importance of this crucial moment in Israel's history.

After the shared meal and the sealing of the covenant, Moses and Joshua were again summoned to the top of Sinai (vv. 12-18). The stated purpose of their going was to receive the tables of stone containing the law (v. 12). Then the glory of the Lord covered the mountain, and Moses was addressed out of the midst of the cloud (v. 16). Moses remained on the mount of revelation forty days and forty nights (v. 18).

7. The Breaking of the Covenant *(31:18 to 32:35)*
Exodus 25:1 to 31:17 covers the instructions Moses received during his prolonged stay on Mount Sinai regarding the construction of the taber-

nacle and its furnishings and the organization of worship in Israel. The historical narrative resumes in 31:18 to 32:35, where we learn of the strange things that went on in the camp of Israel while Moses was away.

During the forty days Moses was on the mountain receiving God's laws and commandments, the people grew tired of waiting for him. They supposed that he had disappeared forever. Since he had left them, they sought to devise some appropriate means of worshiping the God who had delivered them from Egypt.

Aaron seems not to have discouraged the people in their plans. In fact, he collected their offerings of gold and made a calf of gold for them. Israel then bowed down before the golden calf and worshiped it.

This should have been the highest moment in Israel's history. The vow she had taken was far more binding than the marriage vow. God had pledged himself to be her God, and she had pledged her loyalty to him. Unfortunately, however, her performance did not match her pledge. Her life under the covenant was marked by moral failure and infidelity from the very beginning. Before Moses had returned from the mountain with the tables of laws, she had already broken the first of these. It has aptly been stated that the only covenant Israel ever knew was a broken covenant, broken by her disobedience. The wilderness could have been her Garden of Eden, but it proved to be the scene of her fall.

The story of the golden calf shows that Israel wanted a visible symbol of the God who had redeemed her. The error she committed in the making of the calf was in supposing that God's presence could be captured in this manner. Israel wished to have a visible representation of the invisible God, to capture his presence in the golden calf, just as later generations of Israelites tried to capture his presence in the Temple at Jerusalem. God's rejection of all idols and all image-making meant that his presence could not be captured in some object and manipulated to suit human desires. If God had permitted this, Israel's religion would have degenerated to the low level of that of her pagan neighbors. The calf experience suggests a truth clearly enunciated later by Jesus, " 'God is spirit, and those who worship him must worship in spirit and truth' " (John 4:24).

There is a marked similarity between Israel's sin and that of Adam and Eve in the Garden of Eden. In a real sense Exodus 32 is the counterpart to Genesis 3. Both contain an account of temptation and rebellion. In each case the rebellion followed the giving of a command. God commanded Adam not to eat of the tree of the knowledge of good and evil; he commanded Israel not to make graven images (Ex. 20:4-6).

The parallel extends even further, for as God continued to care for Adam after his fall, so he continued to care for his people after their rebellion. The rest of the Old Testament tells how God maintained the covenant, this broken covenant, in spite of Israel's failure and infidelity. "Where sin increased, grace abounded all the more" (Rom. 5:20).

The Lord was so incensed with the people of Israel that he spoke to Moses as he was coming down the mountain and said to him, " 'Your people, whom you brought out of the land of Egypt, have corrupted themselves.' " God no longer assumed responsibility for the people; they were Moses' people, and it had been Moses who had brought them out of Egypt. God was no longer their God, and they were not his people. They were a stiff-necked people, no longer fit to become God's chosen people. God proposed to destroy them and to form a new nation with Moses at the center (32:7-10).

Some men would have been flattered at such a proposal, but not Moses. Upon hearing of God's intention to destroy the people of Israel, Moses became their intercessor before God. He made two appeals, the first to God's concern for his own reputation before the heathen (vv. 11-12). The second appeal was based on the promises made to the fathers, to Abraham, Isaac, and Israel (Jacob's name after Peniel, Gen. 32:28) (v. 13). In the face of such forceful praying, God relented and agreed to give the nation Israel a second chance (v. 14).

To say that God repented means that he changed his mind (Hebrew: *naham*). God's means are flexible, and he may change his course of action whenever the changed situation warrants it. The verb *naham* always has emotional overtones, either of joy or of sorrow. God may change his mind gladly, as here, or sorrowfully, as in the days of Noah when it grieved him that he had made man (Gen. 6:6). Originally this verb was used to describe heavy breathing, such as the labored breathing of a horse that had been driven hard. The verb always retained something of this meaning, even when applied to men or to God. When one repents in this sense, he either sighs within himself, thus expressing sorrow, or heaves a sigh of relief, expressing joy. But while the verb may express either sorrow or joy, the joy is always that which emerges out of sorrow. God "repented" in response to Moses' prayer, not reluctantly, but with a sense of relief. To punish is always his "strange work" (see Isa. 28:21). To pardon is his delight.

The discovery that the people had made the golden calf led Moses to smash the two tables of the law (vv. 15-19). This action symbolized the breaking of the covenant. Moses then melted the golden calf, ground it into powder, and mixed it with the Israelites' drinking water (v. 20). This was probably intended as a form of trial by ordeal, whereby those who drank the water would die if guilty but go unharmed if innocent (see Num. 5:11-28).

After this incident Moses called for those who were on the Lord's side to come to him (vv. 25-26). The sons of Levi rallied to his side, and he sent them through the camp to slay the rebels (v. 27). The number slain is put at three thousand (v. 28). However, the Vulgate reads twenty-three thousand, a reading apparently influenced by 1 Corinthians 10:8. For their loyalty to Moses, the Levites had a special blessing bestowed upon them (v. 29).

Chapter 32 is concluded with one of Moses' greatest prayers of intercession (vv. 30-35). In it he freely acknowledged that Israel had sinned, but asked for divine forgiveness. He had no basis for such a petition, except to offer his life instead of theirs. He was willing to die for those who had distrusted him, complained against him, and accused him of leading them into the wilderness to die. This prayer remained without parallel until one greater than Moses came and prayed, " 'Father, forgive them; for they know not what they do' " (Luke 23:34).

8. The Renewal of the Covenant *(34:1-35)*

This chapter is a continuation of chapter 32. It describes the renewal of the covenant after the golden calf incident.

Moses received a command to make two tables of stone and to take them with him back to the top of Sinai (vv. 1-2). There God would meet him and write upon the tables of stone the same words that were on the first tables.

Moses obeyed the Lord and went up on Mount Sinai with the two tables of stone in his hand (v. 4). There the Lord appeared to him once more in a cloud and proclaimed to him words that were really a commentary on the meaning of the divine name, " 'The Lord, the Lord, a God merciful and gracious, slow to anger, and abounding in steadfast love and faithfulness, keeping steadfast love for thousands, forgiving iniquity and transgression and sin, but who will by no means clear the guilty, visiting the iniquity of the fathers upon the children and the children's children, to the third and the fourth generation' " (vv. 6-7).

It would be difficult to find a clearer statement of the covenant theology of ancient Israel than that given here. Surely Moses' reaction to the proclamation of the divine name was meant to serve as the model for all future generations of Israelites who came to worship at the sanctuary: "Moses made haste to bow his head toward the earth, and worshiped" (v. 8).

The self-revelation of God in chapter 19 had been followed by the giving of the Ten Commandments in chapter 20. In a similar fashion, the proclamation of the divine name and the renewal of the covenant in chapter 34 are followed by another law code, the so-called "Cultic Decalogue," or "Ritual Decalogue" (vv. 12-26). However, it is a misnomer to call this code a decalogue (Greek for "ten words") since it contains at least twelve commandments. Included among these are the original Ten Commandments (v. 28), with expansions of the First (vv. 11-16), the Second (v. 17), and the Fourth (v. 21). The other laws deal mainly with worship, hence the designation of the code as "cultic."

When Moses returned from the mountain, his face radiated rays of light, a reflection of the divine glory he had seen on the mountain (vv. 29-35). To describe the rays of light coming from Moses' face (v. 29), the Hebrew text employs a word meaning "to send forth horns" *(qaran)*. Here "horns" obviously means "rays." However, the Vulgate translation made by Jerome reproduced in Latin the literal sense of the Hebrew. It described Moses with horns projecting from his forehead. In keeping with this translation, Michelangelo later adorned his famous sculpture of Moses with two horns. Thus a mistranslation was forever set in stone!

9. Lessons for Life from the Scriptures
The call of God is not so much a call to privilege as it is a call to service. Israel was called to be a kingdom of priests (19:6). This meant that she was to exercise a priestly ministry on behalf of all nations, interceding for them before God and instructing them in the ways of God.

It is only too clear from the subsequent record that very few Israelites understood their calling in this light. And yet some of the prophets never lost the vision of their nation's missionary responsibility (see Isa. 2:2-4; 19:23-25; 49:5-6; 56:6-8; Zech. 8:20-23). The book of Jonah in particular reminds Israel of her obligation, represented by the pagan city of Nineveh, to the nations.

Because Israel failed in her mission, it was taken from her and entrusted to others (see Matt. 21:33-43). According to 1 Peter 2:9, Israel's mission has now been given to the church. What an awesome responsibility this places upon those who make up the church. Paul warned Christians of the fearful judgment that would come upon them if they failed to fulfill their mission (Rom. 11:17-22).

Israel's experience at Sinai should teach us to show an attitude of

reverence and respect when we approach God. The Israelites were afraid
even to listen to God; they asked Moses to transmit his words to them
(20:18-20). We do not need Moses as our mediator, for we now have
Jesus (1 Tim. 2:5). And yet we can learn from Israel. The people of
Israel never drew near to God without proper respect for his holiness.
And yet we have often been guilty of stressing his love at the expense of
his holiness. Consider the casual and oftentimes irreverent manner in
which we approach God in our worship services. What would have
been the Hebrew reaction to the modern concept of God as "the man
upstairs"?

The new covenant sealed on Calvary supersedes that made at Sinai. Unfortunately, Israel did not live up to her covenant obligations. Only in a
limited sense did she become a kingdom of priests and a holy nation.
Repeatedly she broke the covenant and transgressed the law. Finally,
when the old covenant had been broken beyond repair, God promised
a new covenant (Jer. 31:31-34).

We believe this promise has been fulfilled in Jesus Christ. The new
covenant was sealed in his shed blood. We celebrate the giving of this
covenant each time we partake of the Lord's Supper and recall the
words of our Lord: " 'This cup is the new covenant in my blood. Do
this, as often as you drink it, in remembrance of me' " (1 Cor. 11:25).
In a real sense therefore we celebrate the feast of the new covenant each
time we partake of the Lord's Supper.

------

[1] Harry Thomas Frank, *Discovering the Biblical World* (New York: Harper and Row, Publishers, 1975), p. 61.

[2] G.A.F. Knight, *Law and Grace* (London: SCM Press, Ltd., 1962), p. 25.

[3] Robert Martin-Achard, *A Light to the Nations,* trans. John Penney Smith (Edinburgh: Oliver and Boyd, 1962), pp. 37-40.

[4] Peshitta: An ancient version of the Bible in Syriac.

[5] Targums: An Aramaic translation or paraphrase of a portion of the Old Testament.

[6] R.B.Y. Scott, "A Kingdom of Priests (Exodus XIX.6)," *Oudtestamentische Studien,* 8 (1950), 213-19.

Personal Learning Activities

1. During the year Israel stayed at Sinai three significant events took place. Identify and arrange in order those events from the list below, using *a, b, c, d,* and *e:*
   ___ (1) Israel ceased to complain.
   ___ (2) God appeared to Moses amid convulsions of nature.
   ___ (3) The people accepted voluntarily a covenant with God.
   ___ (4) Moses broke the stone tables of the law.
   ___ (5) The law was given to guide the Israelites in the covenant obligations.
   ___ (6) While the law was being given, the people broke the covenant through idolatry.

2. Two basic kinds of covenants can be found in the Old Testament. The names for these two kinds of covenants are (select two):
   ___ (1) Parity covenant.   ___ (3) Religious covenant.
   ___ (2) Morality covenant.   ___ (4) Suzerainty covenant.

3. Explain the difference in the two covenants you selected. (See the textbook, "The Old Testament Concept of Covenant," this chapter.)

4. As a result of Israel's covenant with God, her obedience to its terms involved a unique relationship with God. God is recorded as having used three phrases to specify that relationship. (Select from below those phrases.)
   ___ (1) My own possession.   ___ (4) A holy nation.
   ___ (2) A kingdom of priests.   ___ (5) A wealthy trader.
   ___ (3) A ruling people.

5. These special designations of Israel meant that God's purpose for Israel was that she become a missionary to the nations: True ___ False ___

6. In 1 Peter 2:9 these same three phrases found in item 4 are used of Christians. According to your response to item 5, what was Peter's meaning in 2:9 as applied to Christians?

7. Match the two lists below, linking event with meaning:
   ___ (1) Israel appeals to Moses to intercede for them.   ___ (a) Symbol of broken covenant.
   ___ (2) Aaron helps the people make a golden calf.   ___ (b) Action breaks covenant between God and Israel.
   ___ (3) Moses breaks the tables of law.   ___ (c) God continues to work his purpose through Israel.
   ___ (4) Moses prays that God   ___ (d) God forgives the sinner

107

spare Israel

_____ (5) Moses receives and Israel accepts the law a second time.

but punishes sin.

_____ (e) Establishes principle of mediation between God and man.

8

The Moral Demand

of the Covenant

Exodus 20:1-17; 20:22 to 23:33

Up to this point in our study of Exodus, we have been concerned mainly with the narrative portions of the book. We come now to a study of the Ten Commandments (20:1-17) and the Book of the Covenant (20:22 to 23:33). It is in the legal portions of the Pentateuch that many readers get bogged down. Part of the difficulty is due to a lurking suspicion that these ancient laws are not relevant to the contemporary world. Paul's affirmation that the Christian is not under law but under grace (Rom. 6:14) has led many to repudiate the legal portions of the Old Testament. However, in our study we will try to show that there is a positive value in the law, even for Christians.

The truth of the matter is that the law truly understood is not opposed to the gospel. Both law and gospel are gifts of God. Just as there can be no faith without works, even so there can be no gospel without laws. The law as interpreted and lived out by Jesus is still valid for our study. We obey this law, not in order that we might earn salvation, but because we have already experienced salvation as the free gift of God (see John 14:15).

The Hebrew word for law is *torah,* which is derived from a root meaning "to throw," "to cast," "to shoot." Its derived meaning is "point out," "show the way," "instruct," "teach." *Torah* has a wider meaning therefore than usually is indicated by the word "law." In its broader range of meaning it includes teaching, instruction, direction, and revelation. In this sense it was a fundamental part of the covenant relationship, for it taught Israel how to live as the people of God.

We err if we believe that the people of the Old Testament regarded the *Torah* as an unbearable burden. If this were so, then how are we to explain the many references to the law as an unparalleled blessing? Consider, for example, Psalms 1 and 119. Psalm 1 congratulates the man whose delight is in the law of the Lord so that he meditates on it day and night (v. 2). Psalm 119 is an alphabetic poem of twenty-two stanzas. Each stanza contains exactly eight verses. There is one stanza for each of the twenty-two letters in the Hebrew alphabet, and all eight verses in a given stanza begin with the same Hebrew letter. The stanzas run from *aleph* to *taw* (Hebrew letters), or, as we would say, from *a* to *z*. One has only to read this long poem to discover the fundamental joy and delight that faithful Israelites felt when they read the law. They could declare with deep sincerity: "Oh, how I love thy law! It is my meditation all the day" (v. 97; see also Ps. 19:7-11).

In the New Testament the law's value is set forth explicitly. For example, Galatians 3:19-24 states that the law serves the spiritual purpose of identifying transgressions. Moreover, it anticipates Christ and prepares us for him. Romans 3:19-20 states, "Through the law comes knowledge of sin." Similar statements on the spiritual work of the law are found in Romans 5:13, 20; 7:7. In Matthew 5:17 Jesus is reported as saying, " 'Think not that I have come to abolish the law and the prophets; I have come not to abolish them but to fulfill them.' "

Of course we must be careful to distinguish between Old Testament law and the oral traditions which the rabbis derived from this law. The Pharisees by the time of Jesus had found 613 laws in the Pentateuch and preached that men should observe them as the framework for the conduct of the whole of life.[1]

Jesus had difficulty with the Pharisees over their view of oral tradition. On one occasion the Pharisees charged Jesus' disciples with having violated the tradition of the elders by not washing their hands before eating. Jesus answered the Pharisees by pointing out that they had substituted the precepts and traditions of men for the commandment of God (Mark 7:1-13). On another occasion Jesus accused the scribes and Pharisees of binding heavy burdens on other men's shoulders, while not lifting them with so much as one of their fingers (Matt. 23:1-4). Jesus did not believe that oral tradition should be assigned a validity equal to that of Old Testament *Torah*.

Jesus illustrated how he had come to fulfill the law by reinterpreting certain of the laws found in the Pentateuch (see Matt. 5:20-48). What Jesus did in each instance was to add to the authority and significance of the older law by internalizing it. Thus he broadened its demands upon the lives of his followers. He was no legalist in his interpretation of the law, for he was always ready to set aside a particular law in obedience to a higher law. Still we must never forget that he came not to destroy the law but to fulfill it.

1. The Ten Commandments *(20:1-17)*

There is wide variation among different religious groups about how the Commandments should be divided. All groups arrive at a total number of ten, but they do it in different ways. Jews divide them thus: the First, 20:2; the Second, 20:3-6; and the Third through the Tenth, 20:7-17. Roman Catholics and Lutherans divide them thus: the First, 20:2-6; the Second, 20:7; the Third, 20:8-11; the Fourth through the Eighth, 20:12-16; the Ninth, 20:17*a*; and the Tenth, 20:17*b*. Following Philo, Josephus, and the early church fathers, all Protestants, except Lutherans, divide them thus: the First, 20:2-3; the Second, 20:4-6; the Third, 20:7; the Fourth, 20:8-11; and the Fifth through the Tenth, 20:12-17.

Recent research has suggested that there may be a similarity in form between the Ten Commandments and certain ancient Near Eastern political treaties. The Hittites left a wealth of such treaties. These have been studied by Old Testament archaeologists and compared with covenant forms in the Old Testament.[2]

Hittite treaties were made between Hittite kings and lesser kings whom they had conquered and made their vassals. These treaties included the following features: (1) a preamble, in which the king who offered the treaty identified himself to his vassal and described previous acts of benevolence on his behalf; (2) the stipulations imposed upon the vassal, chief of which was a strict prohibition against the vassal's making treaties with any other ruler, plus the requirement that the vassal do nothing to provoke strife or civil war within the realm; (3) provision for the preservation of one copy of the treaty by the officiating king and another by the vassal, the latter being brought out from time to time to be reread and reaffirmed in a covenant renewal ceremony; and (4) a list of blessings for the loyal vassal and a list of curses for the rebellious vassal.

The Ten Commandments exhibit certain parallels to this treaty form. In the preamble God identified himself as " 'the Lord your God.' " He then described his previous act of benevolence on Israel's behalf, " 'Who brought you out of the land of Egypt, out of the house of bondage.' " The preamble is followed by the main body of the document, that is, the covenant stipulations. The first of these is that Israel must not enter into covenant with any other gods, " 'You shall have no other gods before me.' " The final commandments in the list are designed to maintain peace and harmony in the kingdom of Israel and to protect the rights of individual Israelites.

Other parallels to the Hittite treaty forms can be seen in the larger context of the Old Testament. The two tables of the law that Moses brought down from Sinai probably were two complete copies of the Ten Commandments. From time to time Israel seems to have reread and reaffirmed the covenant regulations in a covenant renewal ceremony (see Deut. 11:29-30; 27:1-26; 31:9-13; Josh. 8:30-35; 24:1-28). Finally, there are long lists of blessings and curses that will be visited upon Israel in accord with her faithfulness or unfaithfulness to the covenant (see Deut. 27:15 to 28:68).

The particular arrangement of the Ten Commandments, with commandments relating to God coming before those relating to man, is certainly no accident. Throughout the Bible, one's belief about God precedes and forms the foundation for ethics. The order is never reversed. God's identification of himself as Israel's Redeemer justifies the commands that follow. Furthermore, the quality of the relationship between God and man determines the quality of human relationships. The Hebrews would never have subscribed to the notion that what a man believes about God does not matter, so long as he deals justly with his fellowman. They would have affirmed, rather, that justice in human relations is rooted and grounded in belief in God and submission to his claims upon one's life.

The Ten Commandments with their preamble suggest three truths about God. (1) *He is:* " 'I am the Lord your God.' " This is the uniform testimony of the Old Testament: " 'Hear, O Israel: The Lord our God is one Lord' " (Deut. 6:4). (2) *He speaks to men.* Moses heard his voice and conveyed his message to Israel. Since he is a revealing God, it is imperative for us to have a listening heart, to be able to say with Samuel, " 'Speak, Lord, for thy servant hears' " (1 Sam. 3:10). (3) *He gives guidance to men in their daily living.* The Ten Commandments show that God is concerned about man's public and his private life. He lays down guidelines for living. These apply in the Temple, in the home, in the marketplace, in the courtroom—wherever man enters into relationship either with God or with his fellowman. The Commandments say no in order that man may say yes to the will of God. In their original setting they spelled out for Israel what it meant to live as the Lord's "special possession." They furnished a deliberate profile of the "kingdom of priests" and the "holy nation." They made known the specific and concrete will of God that the people had agreed to follow.

As far as literary form is concerned, the Ten Commandments belong to a category known as apodictic, or unconditional, law. They consist of short commands or prohibitions without any specification as to how they are to be implemented. This means that they were regarded as so fundamental that obedience to them was not optional. They were ultimate commands of God representing his absolute demand for an inward and spiritual commitment on the part of his people. The people were not asked whether or not they would like to live under these laws. They were not asked to judge whether or not the laws were reasonable. They were not even asked to discuss whether or not human beings could perfectly observe them. Very simply, but quite emphatically, the laws were presented as divine commands which must be obeyed.

The Ten Commandments provided only the basic framework of Old Testament law. They forbade the worship of other gods, for instance, but did not specify how Israel was to implement her worship of the true God. They forbade murder, but did not specify the penalty for murder. For this reason the Ten Commandments have been referred to as policy legislation, in distinction from procedural legislation. They are the stipulations that defined for Israel what it meant to live under the covenant. The true members of the covenant community were those who did *not* do such acts as those forbidden in the Commandments. The rest of the laws in the Old Testament are an application of the Ten Commandments to all of life—in the home, in the courts, in the marketplace, and in the Temple.

Some people have objected to the Ten Commandments because most of them are stated negatively—"Thou shalt not." However, biblical scholars have been quick to point out that the negative form of the Commandments does not indicate a negative attitude toward life. On the contrary, the negative is the only truly universal form of law. A prohibition forbids action in only one area, leaving all other areas free. A positive command, on the other hand, limits action to a specific area, cutting down on one's freedom of decision and action. The Commandments stated negatively left great leeway for the priests and judges in Israel to apply them to specific issues. It was possible of course for them to be applied in such a way as to make the law a burden rather than a blessing. However, such a development did not arise out of the negative form of the Commandments.

Those people who advocate a society without any prohibitions need to be reminded that in morals as well as in mathematics there is a minus as well as a plus. Some experiences impoverish life, while others enrich it.

The validity of the Ten Commandments has recently been reaffirmed by Donald T. Campbell, a psychologist at Northwestern University. Campbell believes that human beings have a biological bias in favor of self-seeking, uninhibited behavior. To counter this bias, human societies have evolved strong ethical and religious rules favoring the group over the individual. The Ten Commandments and similar laws serve as brakes on too much antisocial behavior. Campbell believes that these ancient precepts might be "better tested than the best of psychology's and psychiatry's speculations on how lives should be lived.' "[3]

The First Commandment (20:2-3)

Verse 2 serves as a preamble to all of the Ten Commandments. It shows that the Commandments are firmly anchored in God's mighty act of deliverance at the Exodus. To quote the Commandments without this preamble would be to distort their meaning. These demands are laid upon God's people because the people are his, and because of the kind of God he is. He introduces himself not as the Creator of heaven and earth, but as the Author of liberty, as the Redeemer who has brought Israel out of Egypt. He would like for Israel to remember him primarily in this role, and remembering this, to love him and obey him.

The First Commandment (v. 3) emphasizes God's demand that he alone be worshiped in Israel. If Israel were to live in covenant with him, she must not enter into covenant with false gods. The ancient world was full of such gods. Shamash was the sun-god. The moon-god was called Sin. Baal was the Canaanite god of fertility, and Astarte was his consort. The pyramid tombs of the pharaohs show how the Egyptians worshiped the Nile River, the sacred bull, and the heavenly bodies. This helps us understand the urgency with which Moses warned the Israelites that these religions were not for them.

God does in fact make totalitarian claims upon his people. James Smart has written of the totalitarian nature of his claims:

> Our God is a jealous God. He will not share the worship of our hearts with anyone or with anything; it must be concentrated upon him alone. . . . When we conceal this uncompromising claim and offer the gifts of God—the good life, forgiveness, peace with God, spiritual security—at a lesser price, we make of our church a kind of bargain counter of salvation. We let family, nation, and all manner of importunate personal

interests take the primary place in men's lives and are
content so long as they are willing to give God a place,
even though it may be a subordinate one, unaware that
we have betrayed our people into a fatal disorder. God
will not take second place.[4]

The Second Commandment (20:4-6)

The purpose of this commandment is clearly to forbid Israel to make or
worship any image of her God. This commandment emphasizes God's
separateness and otherness from all created things. He cannot be visibly
represented by any of them. That archaeologists have never found any
picture, image, or other visual representation of Israel's God in any of
their excavations is an interesting fact. Israel must have obeyed this
command.

The Jews later interpreted the Second Commandment as applying
even to the coins with which they paid the Temple tax. Since Roman
coins bore the image of the Roman emperor, they were considered
unacceptable for use in the Jerusalem Temple. This explains why in the
time of Jesus there were money changers within the Temple precincts.
They were there to assist worshipers in exchanging the forbidden
Roman coins for the special coins issued by the Sanhedrin for use in
the Temple.

The First Commandment limited Israel's worship to one God. The
Second Commandment told Israel that God was to be worshiped without images. No physical likeness of him was to be made, for the Creator
could not be represented by that which he himself had created. A fuller
understanding of this same truth is reflected in the words of Jesus,
" 'God is spirit, and those who worship him must worship in spirit and
truth' " (John 4:24).

A further explanation of the purpose behind the Second Commandment is given in Deuteronomy 4. In Moses' speech to the people of
Israel about the making of the covenant at Sinai, he said, " 'You came
near and stood at the foot of the mountain. . . . Then the Lord spoke
to you out of the midst of the fire; you heard the sound of the words,
but saw no form; there was only a voice. . . . Therefore take good
heed to yourselves. Since you saw no form on the day that the Lord
spoke to you at Horeb out of the midst of the fire, beware lest you act
corruptly by making a graven image for yourselves, in the form of any
figure' " (Deut. 4:11-12, 15-16). The point made in this passage is that
God's unique revelation of himself to Israel came through the spoken
word, not through some visible representation. In this respect he is

sharply distinguished from false gods. These have visible shapes, but they cannot speak (see Ps. 115:3-8). Israel's invisible God had spoken his word to her, " 'Did any people ever hear the voice of a god speaking out of the midst of the fire, as you have heard, and still live?' " (Deut. 4:33). That fact about her God set Israel apart from other nations.

The Third Commandment (20:7)

The Third Commandment protects the divine name Yahweh (Lord) from profane use. However, this is not fundamentally a law against profanity.

A person's name meant much more to the ancient Hebrews than to us. The name stood for the individual himself—his person, his attributes, and his powers. In ancient times it was thought that knowing the name of a deity gave one power over him (see Gen. 32:29). To take the name of God in vain probably included the use of his name in taking a false oath, that is, in perjury. It probably included also the use of his name in incantations, sorcery, and magic. God did not sanction the use of his name for such worthless, empty, and vain purposes. One should not pronounce the name of God loosely or thoughtlessly for any base purpose.

In the course of time, the Jews came to regard this commandment as forbidding any enunciation of the name Yahweh. The fear of misuse finally became the fear of any use at all. The time came when only the high priest might still pronounce the name, and then only on solemn occasions. In all other circumstances the name was replaced by such words as *Elohim* (God) and *Adonai* (Lord). This practice is still observed by most Jews up to the present time.

Concerning the meaning of this commandment, Williams has written: "In effect the commandment says, if you use the name of God, be sure that you mean what you say. It is directed against the priest of Yahweh who lifts up God's name in order to further his own ambitions, against the elder who parades his religion in order to win friends and influence people, against the theologian who has become so accustomed to the name of God that it rolls off his tongue without thought or reverence."[5]

The Fourth Commandment (20:8-11)

The sabbath is first mentioned in the Old Testament in Exodus 16:23, in connection with the giving of the manna. This means that the observance of the sabbath predated the giving of the law at Sinai. This is perhaps indicated also by the first word of the Fourth Commandment,

"Remember."

The law of the sabbath had deep social significance. It was the working man's charter of freedom. The sabbath on the seventh day was meant to bring rest and relaxation from the labor of the six-day week (see Ex. 23:12; 31:12-17). But its purpose went beyond this. Israel was commanded not only to "remember" the sabbath but also to "keep it holy." It was meant not only to bring physical rest to the weary, but also to give sustenance to man's spirit.

The justification for man's keeping the sabbath is given in verse 11. It is rooted in creation. Israel is to observe the sabbath because the Creator himself rested on the seventh day. According to Exodus 31:17, God not only rested on the seventh day, but he was refreshed by his rest. Exodus 23:12 pictures the sabbath as a time when the ox, the ass, the son of a slave, and the alien also rest and are refreshed. Commenting on these passages, Martin Buber has written that this command "binds together the deity and the tired, exhausted slave, and with words arousing the soul calls the attention of the free man's indolent heart to the slave."[6]

The meaning of the sabbath for Christians has been transferred from the seventh day to the first day of the week in celebration of the resurrection of Christ. What a blessed privilege to observe the Lord's Day! When we do so, all of life falls into the rhythmic pattern of meaningful work and festive rest. On this special day out of seven we lay down our strengths and our achievements at the feet of him who created us for his praise and his adoration. In a sense the sabbath expresses the essence of all the other Commandments, both in its religious as well as its social meaning.

The Fifth Commandment (20:12)

Note the significance of the position of this commandment immediately following the four dealing with one's duties toward God. The primary duty in the social sphere is one's duty toward his parents. When this is ignored or abused, the social structure collapses. Note that the mother is included alongside the father as worthy of honor. The underlying assumption of this commandment is that the family, as designed by God, is the foundation of human society. Just as our parents are the first persons to whom we become adjusted, even so our relationship to them will color our relationship to others and also to God. One who is not properly related to his own parents usually finds it difficult to be properly related to God. On the other hand, a child who has learned love from his parents finds it easier to respond to the love of God.

The Fifth Commandment often has been interpreted as having been addressed almost exclusively to small children. However, its primary concern is with the respect due elderly parents residing in the homes of their sons and daughters. The social structure was such in ancient Israel that elderly parents who could no longer work were usually provided for in the homes of their children. Such a system was subject to abuse, and sometimes the aged were treated harshly and denied the support they deserved (see Prov. 19:26; 20:20).

A good example of how men were circumventing the Fifth Commandment in the days of Jesus is furnished by Jesus' words to the scribes and Pharisees, when he said to them, " 'You have a fine way of rejecting the command of God, in order to keep your tradition! For Moses said, "Honor your father and your mother"; and, "He who speaks evil of father or mother, let him surely die"; but you say, "If a man tell his father or his mother, What you would have gained from me is Corban" (that is, given to God)—then you no longer permit him to do anything for his father or mother, thus making void the word of God through your tradition which you hand on' " (Mark 7:9-13).

The Fifth Commandment, as Paul observed (Eph. 6:2), is the first to carry a promise. Parents are to be honored, " 'that your days may be long in the land which the Lord your God gives you.' " The promise attached to this commandment refers not so much to individual longevity as to the longevity and well-being of the entire community. In terms of the twentieth century, it means that when a nation is concerned about the needs of its senior citizens, it is laying the foundation for a stable and enduring society.

The Sixth Commandment (20:13)

The words which God spoke to Israel at Sinai were basically words of freedom. They were prefaced by the divine affirmation: "I am the Lord your God, who brought you out of the land of Egypt, out of the house of bondage' " (20:2). However, Israel's freedom under the covenant was not unlimited. It involved responsibility for the welfare of others. There were certain things that one was not free to do to others. Freedom under the covenant meant that others had certain inalienable rights which could not be violated with impunity.

The Bible teaches respect for human life. Therefore it is forbidden to take the life of another by murdering him. The verb "to kill" should be translated "to murder." Murder was the first crime committed by Adam's children (Gen. 4:8-16). The prohibition of murder was one of the stipulations of the covenant which God made with Noah (Gen. 9:6).

It must be recognized that nowhere in the Bible is capital punishment or the waging of war condemned. But does this mean that we should accept these as positive goods? Or as necessary evils? Is taking the life of a condemned criminal or of one's enemy on the battlefield justifiable killing?

Perhaps the least we can do as Christians is to follow the advice of Elton Trueblood and cultivate an uneasy conscience about the taking of human life under any circumstances. Trueblood has written:

> If it is important to cultivate an uneasy conscience concerning the death or suffering of animals, it is a thousand times more important to cultivate such a conscience in regard to the death or suffering of human beings. It is admitted that some human beings must sometimes die to save other human beings or to save a way of living which will dignify and beautify other lives, some of them as yet unborn. All this we are forced to accept if we are reasonable and not merely sentimental, *but we dare not let ourselves get used to it and therefore take it lightly.*[7]

The Seventh Commandment (20:14)

The second freedom that is restricted by the Ten Commandments is the freedom to commit adultery. The Seventh Commandment recognizes the right of every couple to maintain the sanctity of their marriage.

The Bible regards monogamy, that is, the lifelong union of one man and one woman, as the norm for marriage. This was God's intention from the beginning (see Gen. 2:24; Mark 10:2-9). Adultery is wrong because it undermines God's intention in marriage, and because it brings injury, grief, guilt, and shame to the persons involved (see Prov. 5:3-6; 6:23-29).

The two words most frequently used in the Bible to describe sexual perversion are "adultery" and "fornication." Adultery has reference to sexual relations with another man's wife or fiancée. It is condemned throughout the Bible (see Lev. 18:20; 20:10; Deut. 22:23-24). Fornication (Greek: *porneia,* from which comes the term "pornography") as used in the Old Testament means "to play the harlot." In the New Testament it refers to all sexual relations outside marriage (see Acts 15:20; 1 Cor. 5:1; Gal. 5:19; 1 Thess. 4:3).

The case for sexual purity in the Scriptures is based upon the view that the sexual capacity is a God-given capacity, a blessing too sacred to be abused. Nothing human is more sacred or more meaningful than the love of a man and a woman who have committed themselves to each other for life. We ought to be grateful to God that one of the Commandments is designed to protect the sanctity of such a relationship.

The Eighth Commandment (20:15)

To steal means to take by stealth, that is, to take the property of another without his knowledge. The verb "to steal" may have as its object either a person (see Ex. 21:16; Deut. 24:7) or a thing (Ex. 22:1). This commandment limits the freedom of a person to become a thief. The apostle Paul wrote that the corrective for stealing was honest work (Eph. 4:28).

The Ninth Commandment (20:16)

This commandment protects the right of every man to a fair trial. It forbids the giving of false testimony under oath against one's neighbor. For this reason, Childs has rendered it, " 'You shall not testify against your neighbor as a lying witness.' "[8] Israel's prophets spoke out vigorously against this evil (see Jer. 7:9-10; Hos. 4:2). Nothing so threatens the fabric of society as disregard for the truth in the law courts of the land.

The Tenth Commandment (20:17)

This commandment forbids one to covet that which belongs to his neighbor. However, the verb "to covet" means more than merely to have a secret desire for something that belongs to another. It denotes not only a desire but also the action which stems from the desire (see Ex. 34:24). The covetous man is the one who not only desires his neighbor's possessions but actually takes steps to acquire them for himself. When seen in this light, the Tenth Commandment, like the Eighth, guarantees the fundamental right of private property.

Elton Trueblood has described this body of laws "not [as] an outworn set of specific prohibitions, but positive principles of such a nature that a good society cannot be constructed or reconstructed without reference to them."[9]

2. The Book of the Covenant (20:22 to 23:33)

Included in the book of Exodus is an ancient collection of laws extending from 20:22 to 23:33. The collection is usually referred to as the Book of the Covenant or the Covenant Code. These designations are based on Exodus 24:7: "Then he [that is, Moses] took the book of the covenant, and read it in the hearing of the people; and they said, 'All that the Lord has spoken we will do, and we will be obedient.' " It is likely that the term "Book of the Covenant" originally referred to the Ten Commandments alone and was only later applied to this larger collection of laws.

The Book of the Covenant is recognized as the earliest code of laws in the Pentateuch and one of the oldest known among ancient peoples. It preceded Roman law by at least a thousand years. It is unique both in its origin and in its contents. Its deep sensitivity for morality and justice influenced the development of all subsequent law in Israel. This influence is particularly evident in Deuteronomy 22—24.

The Book of the Covenant in Exodus may be outlined as follows:

1. Laws regulating worship (20:22-26)
   (1) Prohibition of images (20:22-23)
   (2) Instructions regarding altars (20:24-26)
2. Laws protecting human rights (21:1-32)
   (1) The rights of slaves (21:1-11)
   (2) Punishment for bodily injury (21:12-32)
3. Laws protecting property rights (21:33 to 22:17)
   (1) Crimes of carelessness (21:33-36)
   (2) Laws regulating stealing (22:1-4)
   (3) Crimes of neglect (22:5-6)
   (4) Cases involving trusteeship (22:7-15)
   (5) Seduction of a virgin (22:16-17)
4. Miscellaneous social and religious laws (22:18 to 23:9)
   (1) Capital offenses (22:18-20)
   (2) Laws of compassion and piety (22:21-31)
   (3) The demand for justice (23:1-9)
5. A calendar of religious festivals (23:10-19)
   (1) The sabbatical year (23:10-11)
   (2) The sabbath (23:12-13)
   (3) Three annual feasts (23:14-17)
   (4) Sacrifices and offerings (23:18-19)
6. Concluding exhortation (23:20-33)

Several features of this law code merit consideration. The first is its broad humanitarian spirit. It is highly significant that its first laws governing human rights are concerned with the rights of slaves (21:1-11). No other nation in antiquity is known to have included in its law books regulations for the kindly treatment of its slaves. The rules regarding slaves in the Book of the Covenant are unusually merciful, and even go so far as to make provision for the freeing of slaves under certain conditions. Even the slave had rights which his owner was not free to ignore (21:26-27).

The humanitarian spirit is present also in the law of retaliation, "Life for life, eye for eye, tooth for tooth, hand for hand, foot for foot, burn for burn, wound for wound, stripe for stripe" (21:23-25). This law operated to limit retaliation, so that it might not exceed "an eye for an eye, and a tooth for a tooth." In this sense it was a humanitarian law and served a just purpose. Of course this is not to ignore the fact that Jesus articulated a higher law for Christian "revenge" (see Matt. 5:38-42).

The humanitarian spirit can also be seen in the provisions made for the protection of other defenseless members of society besides the slave. Twice the Israelites were commanded to refrain from harming or oppressing the stranger living in their midst, remembering that they once were strangers in the land of Egypt (22:21; 23:9). Neither were they permitted to mistreat any widow or orphan, lest God's wrath be loosed against them with the consequence that their wives become widows and their children orphans (22:22-24). They were commanded to lend to a poor man without charging him interest. If they took his coat as collateral for such loans, they were to return it to him before nightfall, so that he could cover himself with it while he slept (22:25-27). Even the command to keep the sabbath is based upon a humanitarian motive: "Six days you shall do your work, but on the seventh day you shall rest; that your ox and your ass may have rest, and the son of your bondmaid, and the alien, may be refreshed" (23:12; see also Deut. 5:14-15).

A second feature of the Book of the Covenant is its demand for justice in human affairs. A typical section exhibiting this concern is 23:1-3: " 'You shall not utter a false report. You shall not join hands with a wicked man, to be a malicious witness. You shall not follow a multitude to do evil; nor shall you bear witness in a suit, turning aside after a multitude, so as to pervert justice; nor shall you be partial to a poor man in his suit.' " Or consider 23:6-8: " 'You shall not pervert the justice due to your poor in his suit. Keep far from a false charge, and do not slay the innocent and the righteous, for I will not acquit the wicked. And you shall take no bribe, for a bribe blinds the officials, and subverts the cause of those who are in the right.' "

A third prominent feature of this law code is its long list of crimes which are punishable by death. One could be put to death for murder (21:12), for assault with deadly intent (21:14), for striking or cursing father or mother (21:15,17), or for kidnapping another (21:16). If one let his ox run free when it was known beforehand to be dangerous, and if it gored a man or woman to death, then both the ox and its owner were to be stoned to death (21:29). Sorcery, sexual perversion, and idolatry were also punishable by death (22:18-20). These were harsh measures designed to purge the Israelites from evil and to prepare them to be the people of God.

A fourth important feature of the Book of the Covenant is its concern with matters related to worship. It prohibits the making of gods of silver and gods of gold (20:23). Specific instructions are given for the constructing of altars (20:24-26).

Of special interest is the provision that all male members of the community appear before the Lord three times each year in order to keep a feast to him (23:14-17). These included the Feast of Unleavened Bread, the Feast of Harvest, and the Feast of Ingathering. These are also known as Passover, Pentecost, and Tabernacles, respectively (see Ex. 34:18-23; Lev. 23:1-44; Deut. 16:16-17). The Book of the Covenant emphasized that no one was to appear before the Lord empty-handed, but each was to bring an offering of the firstfruits of his labor whenever he came to worship (23:15-16,19).

The Book of the Covenant concludes with a list of blessings that were promised Israel if she were obedient (23:20-33). She would be rescued from her enemies: " 'I will be an enemy to your enemies and an adversary to your adversaries' " (v. 22). " 'I will send my terror before you, and will throw into confusion all the people against whom you shall come, and I will make all your enemies turn their backs to you' " (v. 27). She would also be blessed with health, prosperity, and long life: " 'You shall serve the Lord your God, and I will bless your bread and your water; and I will take sickness away from the midst of you. None shall cast her young or be barren in your land; I will fulfill the number of your days' " (vv. 25-26).

3. Lessons for Life from the Scriptures

The law of the Old Testament is to be rightly understood as one of God's good gifts to his people. Israel's unique status as the recipient of the law is succinctly stated in Deuteronomy 4:8, " 'What great nation is there, that has statutes and ordinances so righteous as all this law which I set before you this day?' "

This verse reminds us of the words of Paul as recorded in Romans 3:1-2: "Then what advantage has the Jew? . . . Much in every way. To begin with, the Jews are entrusted with the oracles of God."

Throughout the Old Testament the law is pictured not as a burden upon Israel, but as a gift of divine grace. Israel was commanded not to add to this law nor to take from it (Deut. 4:2). In other words, she was not to fit the law to herself, but she was to fit herself to the law. If she obeyed this law, she would dwell long in the land which the Lord her God was giving to her.

Christian liberty does not mean license, since life must still be regulated by law. It would be a stupid and fatal mistake for us to suppose that we no longer needed the law of God to guide us in our daily living.

The following story illustrates our need for a fixed point of reference, for a signpost along life's way. The skipper of a small boat had taken on an inexperienced deckhand. One night at sea the skipper grew sleepy. Leaving the new crewman at the wheel, he went below to take a nap. Before he left, he pointed out the North Star and cautioned the crewman to keep the boat headed in that direction. After a while, however, the crewman also grew drowsy and fell asleep at the wheel. When he awoke, he was hopelessly lost. He looked for the North Star but couldn't find it anywhere. Finally, in desperation, he went to the skipper, woke him up, and said, "Please sir, could you come and show me another star to guide by? I think I've passed the other one!"

In this day of relative morality and situational ethics, there are many who insist that we no longer need the Word of God to guide us. They think the world has outgrown the Ten Commandments. But could it be that having abandoned the law of God as our point of reference, we are simply lost and adrift on the sea of life? We don't need a new star to guide us. We just need to get our bearings and to set our course by the star that has been there all along.

Words that Moses addressed to Israel long ago are still appropriate in our situation: " 'This commandment which I command you this day is not too hard for you, neither is it far off. It is not in heaven, that you should say, "Who will go up for us to heaven, and bring it to us, that we may hear it and do it?" Neither is it beyond the sea, that you should say, "Who will go over the sea for us, and bring it to us, that we may hear it and do it?" But the word is very near you; it is in your mouth and in your heart, so that you can do it' " (Deut. 30:11-14). That Paul quoted portions of these verses in connection with the gospel's proclamation and a faith response to them is significant for the Christian. (See Rom. 10:5-17.) Through faith in Christ the believer has the indwelling Holy Spirit given him. The Spirit helps the believer and sets him "free from the law of sin and death" (Rom. 8:2). By following the edicts of the Spirit we do more than fulfill the law; we produce the

Spirit's fruit in our lives (Gal. 5:16-25).

Jesus taught that the essence of the law lies in love for God and love for one's neighbor. Donald Gowan has shown how important Jesus' teaching is when seen against its Jewish background:

> Other teachers had found ways to summarize the essence of these [Mosaic] commandments: David reduced them to eleven, in Psalm 15; Isaiah to six (Isa. 33:15-16); Micah to three (Mic. 6:8); Isaiah again to two (56:1); then Amos and Habakkuk reduced them to one ('seek me and live' in Amos 5:4, and 'the just shall live by faith' in Hab. 2:4). We cannot help comparing the similar activity of Jesus in summing up the whole law in the two-fold law of love—for God and for one's neighbor (quoting Deut. 6:5 and Lev. 19:18; Matt. 22:34-40).[10]

———

[1]Knight, *op. cit.,* p. 52.

[2]Raymond E. Brown, *The Book of Deuteronomy* (Collegeville: The Liturgical Press, 1965), pp. 114-22.

[3]Donald T. Campbell, "Morals Make a Comeback," *Time,* 15 September 1975, p. 94.

[4]James D. Smart, *The Old Testament in Dialogue with Modern Man* (Philadelphia: The Westminster Press, 1964), p. 70.

[5]Jay G. Williams, *Ten Words of Freedom* (Philadelphia: Fortress Press, 1971), p. 137.

[6]Martin Buber, *The Prophetic Faith* (New York: Harper & Row, 1949), p. 54.

[7]Elton Trueblood, *Foundations for Reconstruction* (New York: Harper and Brothers, 1946), p. 67.

[8]Childs, *op. cit.,* p. 424.

[9]Trueblood, *op. cit.,* p. 10.

[10]Donald E. Gowan, *The Triumph of Faith in Habakkuk* (Atlanta: John Knox Press, 1976), p. 11.

Personal Learning Activities

1. The arrangement of the Ten Commandments places man's duty to God before his duty to his fellowman. From the list below indicate that statement which most accurately explains the reason for that arrangement:
   ____ (1) This arrangement reflects a Hittite treaty form.
   ____ (2) This arrangement signifies the importance to man and his society his understandings about God.
   ____ (3) This arrangement is merely accidental.

2. The Ten Commandments suggest three truths about God which are stated in the sentences below. Complete each sentence by supplying the missing word:
   (1) He _____ .
   (2) He _____ to men.
   (3) He gives _____ to men in their daily living.

3. Complete the following sentence about the Ten Commandments by the insertion of the words yes and no:
   "The Commandments say _____ in order that man may say _____ to the will of God."

4. The negative is used in all but two of the Commandments because (select correct response):
   ____ (1) God mistrusts human beings.
   ____ (2) Man cannot handle freedom.
   ____ (3) God wishes to prohibit specific actions, leaving all other possible actions free.

5. The Ten Commandments are designed to (select one):
   ____ (1) Protect individual freedom at the expense of society.
   ____ (2) Curb individual self-seeking as protection for society.

6. Certain characteristics mark the Book of the Covenant in Exodus. From the statements below select those which are mentioned in the textbook:
   ____ (1) The humanitarian spirit.
   ____ (2) A demand for justice in human affairs.
   ____ (3) A demand for death as punishment for numerous crimes.
   ____ (4) A concern for matters related to worship.

Answers:

1. (2); 2. *is, speaks, guidance;* 3. *no, yes;* 4. (3); 5. (2); 6. All responses.

9

God's Presence

with His Pilgrim People
Exodus 33; 35—40

A summary of the chronology of the Exodus events will better prepare us to understand the material in this passage. The Exodus itself occurred in the first month of the first year, on the fourteenth day of the month (Ex. 12:2-6,17-18). On the third new moon after the Exodus, the Israelites arrived at Mount Sinai (19:1). Three days later the covenant-making ceremony took place (19:16). After this the Lord summoned Moses to the top of Mount Sinai, where he remained forty days and forty nights, receiving the tables of the law and the instructions for building the tabernacle and for organizing the worship of Israel (24:12 to 31:18). When Moses came down the mountain and saw the golden calf the people had made during his absence, he broke the tables of the law to symbolize the broken covenant (32:19). He was then summoned back to the mountaintop where he stayed another forty days and forty nights, during which the covenant was renewed and the tables of law rewritten (34:27-28). Coming down the mountain again, Moses assembled the people and gave them instructions for building the tabernacle (35:1-19). The people then set to work, and the tabernacle was finished on the first day of the first month of the second year (40:17). The people left Sinai and headed north toward Canaan on the twentieth day of the second month of the second year (Num. 10:11-12). Thus it had taken them three months to reach Sinai, and their sojourn at Sinai lasted about eleven months.

Why was it necessary for the Israelites to remain so long at Sinai, and what were they doing all this time? The answer to these questions is given in Exodus 33 and in two lengthy parallel sections in Exodus

25—31 and 35—40. The Israelites extended their stay at Sinai in order to complete the construction of the tabernacle and its furnishings.

But, we might ask, why was the tabernacle so important? Why were thirteen chapters, well over a fourth of the book of Exodus, devoted to this subject alone? The answer involves what was to the Israelites a pressing problem. God had rescued them from Egypt and brought them as on eagles' wings to meet him at Sinai (19:4). At this sacred mountain they had experienced his awesome presence and had entered into a solemn covenant with him. There they had received the tables of stones to guide them in fulfilling their covenant obligations. Sinai had indeed become sacred ground to them.

But they could not remain at Sinai forever. Soon they must head northward and claim the inheritance that God had promised to their forefathers, to Abraham, to Isaac, and to Jacob. Their ultimate destination was Canaan, far to the north of Sinai.

The problem facing the Israelites as they thought of leaving Sinai was how they were to maintain contact with the God of Sinai. Was he confined to this mountain of revelation as the gods of other nations were restricted to their particular locales? Would it be necessary for them to make annual pilgrimages back to his dwelling place?

The solution to this problem came in the form of the instructions given to Moses to construct the tabernacle. This portable tent was a sign of God's continuing presence with his pilgrim people. It is not surprising therefore that one Old Testament scholar has referred to the construction of this desert sanctuary by Moses and the Israelites as "the goal of the Priestly history."[1]

The book of Exodus concludes with the supreme object and benefit of the covenant relationship described as the new nearness of God to his people by means of the tabernacle. Moses gave classic expression to this truth when he said to God, " 'If thy presence will not go with me, do not carry us up from here. For how shall it be known that I have found favor in thy sight, I and thy people? Is it not in thy going with us, so that we are distinct, I and thy people, from all other people that are upon the face of the earth?' " (Ex. 33:15-16). This passage might well be regarded as the most important in the Old Testament for understanding the significance of the covenant-presence of the Lord with his people. It was the divine presence in her midst more than anything else that constituted Israel a nation and that distinguished her from all other nations.

The word "tabernacle" means "tent," or "dwelling place." Its Hebrew form is *mishkan,* derived from the verb *shakan,* "to encamp," or "to tent." Various other names are also given to it in the Old Testament. It is called "the tent of meeting" (Ex. 27:21), "the tabernacle of the testimony" (Ex. 38:21), "the tabernacle of the Lord" (Num. 16:9), and "a sanctuary" (Ex. 25:8). Because God is said to dwell *(shakan)* in the midst of his people (Ex. 25:8; 29:45; Num. 35:34; Ezek. 43:7), postbiblical Judaism coined the expression "Shekinah," or "Shekinah Glory," to designate his earthly presence. Although the term "Shekinah" does not occur in the Old Testament, the concept behind it is represented by the wilderness tabernacle *(mishkan)*.

The general view of the Old Testament is that the Lord's permanent dwelling place is in heaven, but he "tabernacles" *(shakan)*, or "tents," with men. The portable desert tent symbolized this idea. Note in this connection that long after the period of desert wandering had ended and the ark had been deposited in the Temple, the poles by which it had been carried were still permanently attached to it (see 1 Kings 8:8). In the words of Martin Buber, Israel's God was "a great deity of the road."[2] He did not dwell on Mount Sinai, but journeyed with his pilgrim people.

1. The Promise of the Lord's Presence *(33:1-23)*
After the episode of the golden calf (Ex. 32), the Lord commanded Moses to depart from Sinai and to lead the people of Israel to the land promised to their forefathers (33:1-2). The command to leave Sinai brought the question of the Lord's continuing presence with his people into sharp focus.

There were two factors that made this subject a burning issue at this point in history. The first was Israel's concept of the transcendence of God. She had witnessed his awesome self-revelation on Mount Sinai. That revelation had been accompanied by fire, smoke, lightning, thunder, and earthquake. Upon seeing these mighty convulsions in nature, the people were afraid (20:18-19). They fled from the divine presence and requested Moses to act as their mediator, so that they would be spared another such encounter with God. They had also been told that this God was of such a nature that his presence could not be captured in images or idols (20:4-6). Israel had every reason to stand in awe before the transcendence of God.

The question posed by the transcendence of God was related to his immanence. How could this desert God, whose presence could not be captured in images or idols, dwell in a house made with hands? Or, to pose the question in a different way, how could the Lord be present with Israel without in some way limiting his freedom and compromising his majesty?

The second factor bearing upon the subject of God's presence with Israel was Israel's sin and rebellion. Before Moses had returned from the mountain of revelation with the tables of the law, Israel had already broken the first two of these laws. She had made a golden calf and had bowed down to it. The only covenant Israel ever knew was a broken covenant, broken by her sin and rebellion. The problem posed by her rebellion was how she could endure the presence of the holy God in her midst without being totally consumed.

These questions are dealt with in chapter 33 of Exodus. Any study of the covenant-presence of God in the Old Testament should properly begin with this chapter. In his commentary on Exodus, Martin Noth[3] observes that the various textual units of this chapter are held together by the theme of the presence of God in the midst of his people.

The chapter begins with God's command to Moses to depart from Sinai and to journey to Canaan (vv. 1-2). This command links the forthcoming entry into Canaan with the promise made to the patriarchs long ago. The Exodus and the conquest are treated as the continuation of the history that began with Abraham, Isaac, and Jacob, and as the fulfillment of the promises made to them.

God's command is followed by a promise that he will not totally forsake his people (vv. 2-3). He will accompany them in the person of his angel (v. 2; see 32:34). The angel represented God's presence with his people, but was distinguished from God himself. If God had personally accompanied his sinful people, his holiness would have consumed them (vv. 3,5). A constant theme of this chapter is that man cannot see God and live (v. 20).

Upon hearing that God himself would not go from Sinai with them, the people of Israel stripped themselves of their ornaments (vv. 4,5,6). This was a sign of repentance and mourning. The ornaments must have been associated with the worship of a foreign god. The implication of the passage is that the removal of the ornaments would have made it possible for God to accompany them.

Verses 7-11 describe a "tent of meeting" that existed in the Exodus period prior to the building of the tabernacle. The tent of meeting was very simple in comparison with the tabernacle. It was located outside the camp (v. 7), whereas the tabernacle was in the midst of the camp (25:8; Num. 2:1-2). The tent of meeting was attended by Joshua alone (33:11), whereas the tabernacle was served by the Aaronite priests (40:12-14). The tent of meeting served primarily as a place to which Moses withdrew when he wished to seek a word from the Lord. This passage stresses the unique relationship that existed between God and Moses. Moses was a man to whom God spoke "face to face, as a man speaks to his friend" (33:11).

The remainder of chapter 33 (vv. 12-23) is concerned with three requests that Moses directed to God. First, he asked for an experienced person to accompany Israel as their guide in their journey across the desert (v. 12). Moses was unfamiliar with the territory between Sinai and Canaan, and thus felt the need for a more experienced person to go with him. God's answer to this request is given in Numbers 10:29-33. The man given to guide the Israelites was Hobab the Midianite, a man who was at home in the desert.

The second request of Moses was more urgent. It is stated in verses 15 and 16: "He said to him, 'If thy presence will not go with me, do not carry us up from here. For how shall it be known that I have found favor in thy sight, I and thy people? Is it not in thy going with us, so that we are distinct, I and thy people, from all other people that are upon the face of the earth?' " It is generally agreed that the response to this request is recorded in verse 14, "He said, 'My presence will go with you, and I will give you rest.' "

The word used here to describe the divine presence is *panim,* translated "face," or "presence." It is one of the four terms under which the divine presence is usually manifested in the Old Testament. The other three are the "glory," the "angel of the Lord," and "name." For God's presence to go with Israel meant that Israel would not have to make pilgrimages back to Sinai in order to worship him.

Moses' third request was that he be permitted to see God's glory (vv. 18-23). "Glory" (Hebrew: *kabod*) is that which reflects an individual's weight, honor, and wealth. When used of God, it refers to his power and holiness. God's glory usually appears in the Old Testament as a bright light or a burning fire. It is also enveloped in a cloud in order to protect the eyes of the beholder from its burning brightness. The glory therefore both conceals God and reveals God. It represents all of God that human eyes are able to behold, but it is an eloquent witness to the fact that there is more that cannot be seen.

The Lord responded to Moses' request by placing him in the cleft of the rock, which was perhaps a small cave in the side of Mount Sinai. There the hand of the Lord covered Moses as the glory of the Lord passed by (vv. 21-22). After the glory had passed by, the hand was removed, and Moses was permitted to see the back of God, but not his face (v. 23).

It is highly significant that the revelation of the glory of the Lord was accompanied by the proclamation of the divine name. God said to Moses, " 'I will make all my goodness pass before you, and will proclaim before you my name "The Lord"; and I will be gracious to whom I will be gracious, and will show mercy on whom I will show mercy' " (v. 19; see 34:6-7). It was the proclamation of the name that gave substance and meaning to the revelation of the glory.

Commenting on the significance of Moses' vision, W.B.J. Martin has written:

> So Moses is using here the least inadequate words he can find—'back', 'face', 'hands', knowing as well as you and I do that they are all metaphors, symbols, pointers rather than exact descriptions. And what he is striving to say is more important than how he says it. . . . What he is saying is: 'We never see God coming, we only see Him going'. He is saying what Kierkegaard said—that life must be lived forward, but it is only understood backward. We are always wise after the event. While the event is still proceeding, we are unaware of what is going on. Only as we reflect upon it does it strike us that God was in it all along.[4]

2. The Tabernacle of the Lord *(35:1 to 40:38)*

A bleak desert separated Mount Sinai from the land of Canaan. The Israelites were destined to wander in this desert almost forty years before crossing the Jordan into Canaan. They would never have survived the years of wilderness wanderings had not God accompanied them and watched over them by day and by night. The symbol of his presence in their midst was the tabernacle. The significance of the tabernacle is nowhere more clearly stated than in God's words to Moses as recorded in Exodus 29:43-46: " 'There I will meet with the people of Israel, and it shall be sanctified by my glory; I will consecrate the tent of meeting and the altar; Aaron also and his sons I will consecrate, to serve me as priests. And I will dwell among the people of Israel, and will be their God. And they shall know that I am the Lord their God, who brought them forth out of the land of Egypt that I might dwell among them; I am the Lord their God.' "

According to the Exodus account, Moses spent forty days and forty nights on Mount Sinai receiving the instructions for building the tabernacle (24:18; 25:1 to 31:17). There God showed him the form of the tabernacle with all its furnishings (25:9,40; 26:30; 27:8).

The actual construction of the tabernacle was delayed by the golden calf episode (Ex. 32). However, after another period of forty days and forty nights on the mountain, Moses came back down to the camp of the Israelites, bringing with him the tables of the law (Ex. 34:27-28). He then assembled the people and gave them the instructions he had previously received for the building of the tabernacle (35:1-19).

The first reference in the Bible to a freewill offering being collected is in Exodus 35:4-9. Moses needed a vast array of materials for the building of the tabernacle and its furnishings. The only way to secure these materials was to appeal to the generosity of the people themselves. And so Moses launched the first campaign to raise a building fund. From first to last in this campaign, emphasis was placed on the freewill nature of the offerings. " 'Whoever is of a generous heart, let him bring the Lord's offering' " (v. 5). "They came, every one whose heart stirred him, and every one whose spirit moved him, and brought the Lord's offering" (v. 21). "They came, both men and women; all who were of a willing heart" (v. 22). "All the men and women, the people of Israel, whose heart moved them to bring anything for the work which the Lord had commanded by Moses to be done, brought it as their freewill offering to the Lord" (v. 29).

In fact, the response of the people to Moses' appeal was so overwhelming that those in charge of the work finally had to go to Moses and ask him to request the people not to bring any more (36:2-7). What pastor has not dreamed of a response like that from his own congregation!

Moses issued a call not only for building materials but also for skilled craftsmen to undertake the actual building of the tabernacle and its furnishings (35:30 to 36:3). Bezalel and Oholiab were chosen to supervise the work. Once again the freewill nature of their response is emphasized: "Moses called Bezalel and Oholiab and every able man in whose mind the Lord had put ability, every one whose heart stirred him up to come to do the work" (36:2).

Other qualifications besides a willing spirit were demanded of those in charge of the work of construction. Moses outlined these in his speech to the congregation of Israel: " 'See, the lord has called by name Bezalel the son of Uri, son of Hur, of the tribe of Judah; and he has filled him with the Spirit of God, with ability, with intelligence, with knowledge, and with all craftsmanship. . . . And he has inspired him to teach' " (35:30-31,34).

It is clear that the writer of Exodus thought of the construction of the ark as nothing less than an act of worship. In preparation for the work Bezalel was filled with the Spirit of God. And in the broader description of his qualifications we can see what the Lord requires of those who would worship and serve him. He requires the skill of their hands, the intelligence of their minds, the willingness of their hearts, and their readiness to teach others.

The construction of the tabernacle with its furnishings and the preparation for its function as a center of worship involved the following steps: (1) the construction of the tabernacle (36:8-38); (2) the making of the ark and the mercy seat (37:1-9); (3) the making of the table of shewbread (37:10-16); (4) the making of the golden lampstand (37:17-24); (5) the making of the altar of incense (37:25-28); (6) the preparation of the holy anointing oil and incense (37:29); (7) the building of the altar of burnt offerings (38:1-7); (8) the making of the laver of bronze (38:8); (9) the erection of the court of the tabernacle (38:9-20); (10) the making of the priestly garments (39:1-31); (11) the inspection of the tabernacle and all its furnishings and the blessing of the people who had done the work (39:32-43); (12) the erection of the completed tabernacle and the location of the furnishings in their places (40:1-33); and (13) the filling of the tabernacle with the glory of the Lord (40:34-38).

The tabernacle itself had the form of a tent within a tent. The outer tent was made of curtains of goats' hair (36:14). The inner tent, that is, the tabernacle proper, was made of curtains of "fine twined linen and blue and purple and scarlet stuff, with cherubim skillfully worked" (36:8). These curtains of linen were stretched over a frame consisting of bars of acacia wood overlaid with gold (36:20,34).

The tabernacle proper, which was surrounded by an open court, was divided into two sections—the outer "holy place" and the inner "most holy place." They were separated by an elaborate veil (26:33-34).[5] The holy place measured 20 x 10 x 10 cubits, that is, 30 x 15 x 15 feet. The most holy place measured 10 x 10 x 10 cubits, or 15 x 15 x15 feet, which was exactly half the dimensions of the holy of holies in Solomon's Temple (see 1 Kings 6:20; Ezek. 41:4). The perfect cube has always been considered one of the most pleasing forms of architectural art. The symmetry of these dimensions reflected the harmony and perfection of Israel's God and of his dwelling place on earth. In Revelation 21:16 it is stated that the New Jerusalem will be a city that lies foursquare, its length and breadth and height being the same.

Inside the most holy place was the ark of the covenant, an oblong chest of acacia wood overlaid within and without with gold (25:10-22; 37:1-9). It measured 2½ x 1½ x 1½ cubits, or 3¾ x 2¼ x 2¼ feet. It contained the tables of the law, a jar of manna, and Aaron's rod that budded. Covering the ark was a solid slab of gold engraved with cherubim. This lid to the ark was known as the "mercy seat," or "propitiatory." The ark with its mercy seat was a striking symbol of God's nearness to his people: " 'There I will meet with you, and from above the mercy seat, from between the two cherubim that are upon the ark of the testimony, I will speak with you of all that I will give you in commandment for the people of Israel' " (25:22). The ark was actually thought of as the throne of the invisible Lord. This gave rise to the Old Testament description of the Lord as the one who "sits enthroned above the cherubim" (1 Sam. 4:4; 2 Sam. 6:2; 1 Chron. 13:6; Ps. 99:1; Isa. 37:16).

The most holy place contained only the ark of the covenant. The holy place contained three objects: the altar of incense, the golden lampstand, and the table of shewbread. In the enclosed court surrounding the tabernacle were located the altar of burnt offerings and the bronze laver.

The tabernacle and its furnishings were made of various kinds of metal, wood, and cloth. The nearer an object was to the divine presence in the holy of holies, the costlier and more beautiful it was. Ordinary materials, such as bronze and the more common kinds of cloth, were reserved for the objects farthest removed from the holy of holies.

One of the most recent studies of Hebrew weights was made by R.B.Y. Scott.[6] Scott reckoned the talent at about 64 pounds, and the sanctuary shekel at 1/3 ounce, or 9.7 grams. According to this calculation, the tabernacle and its furnishings required approximately 1,900 pounds of gold, 6,347 pounds of silver, and 4,522 pounds of bronze, or a total of over six tons of metal.

Modern readers tend to avoid this section of the Bible with its detailed description of altars and curtains, of cubits and cubicles. Another response is to allegorize everything connected with the tabernacle, and so distort its meaning. We should avoid both of these extremes. We need to be reminded that the author's attention to these minute details reflected his theology. He believed that the tabernacling presence of God with the people of Israel was the single most important fact of their existence. It was this fact alone that made them a distinct and unique people. And the wilderness tabernacle served as the center and symbol of the divine presence. Against this background the extraordinary attention given to the tabernacle is fully understandable.

Attention is also given in Exodus to the priests who were to minister at the tabernacle. Chapter 29 is devoted in its entirety to the instructions regarding their ordination which Moses received while on the mountain. The record of the carrying out of these instructions is found in Leviticus 8:1-36.

Moses was commanded to ordain Aaron and his sons to serve as priests (29:8,9,35). The Hebrew employs an idiom for the act of ordination, which, translated literally, means "to fill the hands." The origin of the idiom is uncertain and its precise meaning is unclear. It may have originated in a ceremony like that described in Exodus 29:22-24 and Leviticus 8:22-29. There it is said that Moses placed in the hands of Aaron and his sons parts of a sacrifice, waved them as a wave offering before the Lord, and then took them from their hands and offered them upon the altar. The "ram of ordination" (29:26) is literally "the ram of filling." Regardless of how the idiom originated, it came to be used in the sense of appointing one to the priesthood and installing him in his office.

The priests were "consecrated" to their office (29:1). This means they were set apart from common tasks in order that they might perform their priestly duties. They were washed with water (29:4) and anointed with oil (29:7). A bull and two rams were offered in sacrifice during the ordination ceremony. The bull served as a sin offering (29:1,10-14), and the first of the rams as a burnt offering (29:15-18). The second ram, the "ram of ordination," was offered as a peace offering (29:28), which means that parts of it were eaten by the priests (29:31-34).

A special part of the ceremony of ordination involved the blood of the ram of ordination. Moses was commanded to take part of the blood and put it on the tips of the priests' right ears, on the thumbs of their right hands, and on the big toes of their right feet (29:20). A similar ceremony, involving both oil and blood, was performed in the cleansing of lepers (see Lev. 14:14,17). The words used by A. Dillman in explaining the meaning of this ceremony have been quoted by Hyatt, "The priest must have consecrated ears to listen at all times to God's holy voice, consecrated hands continually to do holy works, and consecrated feet always to walk in holy ways."[7]

Careful attention was also given to the garments to be worn by Aaron and his sons while they ministered before the Lord in the tabernacle. "Of the blue and purple and scarlet stuff they made finely wrought garments, for ministering in the holy place; they made the holy garments for Aaron; as the Lord had commanded Moses" (39:1; see 28:2-4). The garments included an ephod, which was an apronlike garment of linen designed to be worn whenever the priests appeared be-

fore the Lord (39:2-7; see 28:31-35). A bejeweled breastpiece of ex-
quisite beauty was worn over the ephod (39:8-21). There were also
robes with bells of gold and pomegranates around the skirts
(39:22-26), as well as coats woven of fine linen (39:27-29). For Aaron
alone there was a turban of fine linen (28:38). Fastened to the front of
the turban was a plate of solid gold bearing the inscription, "Holy to
the Lord" (39:30-31; see 28:36-37). This inscription signified that
Aaron the priest, and through him all Israel, belonged to the Lord.
They were set apart for his service.

The special garment made to be worn by the priests were but the out-
ward symbols of the inner consecration that ought to characterize
God's ministers in all ages. Concerning this consecration, J. Edgar
Park has written:

> The real priest is characterized by a deep and growing
> secret religious life, by the common virtues such as are
> admired by all men, and by a love for men and a real
> touch with God. . . . By meditation and long practice
> he has attained skill in prayer, in the attainment of an in-
> fectiously healthy inner life, in influencing the lives of
> others through sympathy and insight. He seeks nothing
> for himself; and for his church he asks only that it be
> judged by its fruits in producing good people, fairly criti-
> cized for its failings. . . . These are the real sacred gar-
> ments of the priesthood; breastpieces, ephods, robes, tur-
> bans, and girdles are nothing if they are not the outward
> signs of these inner graces, and they are a very poor
> substitute for them.[8]

The ceremony of ordination and appointment of Aaron and his sons
to the priesthood lasted seven days (29:35-37). When all this had been
accomplished according to the instructions given to Moses, a wonderful event took place: "Then the cloud covered the tent of meeting, and
the glory of the Lord filled the tabernacle" (40:34). The glory of the
Lord was the visible sign of the Lord's presence with his people. It had
previously appeared on Mount Sinai (Ex. 24:15-17). Now it had come
to fill the tabernacle with a celestial brightness. The awesome appearance of the glory of the Lord in the tabernacle was nothing less
than the fulfillment of the ancient promises to the patriarchs that the
Lord would be Israel's God. When the people of Israel saw this
wondrous sight, they were assured that God was indeed in their midst.

And they knew that his presence would not leave them, but would accompany them as they left Sinai and journeyed toward Canaan (40:36-38).

For us, the description of how God tabernacled with Israel in the wilderness is surpassed by the Gospel accounts of how God pitched his tent among us in the person of his Son. "The Word became flesh and dwelt [literally, 'tented'] among us, full of grace and truth; we have beheld his glory, glory as of the only Son from the Father" (John 1:14). "The law was given through Moses; grace and truth came through Jesus Christ" (John 1:17).

3. Lessons for Life from the Scriptures

The reality and presence of the living God make life most meaningful. Those who would follow God are not promised an easy life. They are not promised wealth or success or the applause of men. They are promised a blessing far greater than any of these, the abiding presence of the living God.

Two defective ideas about God are common among us nowadays. One of these sees God as no more than the original Creator of the universe, who, when he had finished his work, laid his tools aside and walked away. This view sees no continuing dependence of the creation on the Creator. There is no vision of God's continuing power sustaining the universe and holding it in place.

The second view goes a little further, but not far enough. It sees God as only an occasional visitor to the world he created. He intervenes from time to time in the world's affairs, and then withdraws again. The onward course of world events is temporarily halted, and then allowed to go on as usual.

Neither of these views would have made sense to the people of Israel. Their view was that God was eternally present with them. They saw his hand in everything that happened to them, the good as well as the bad. Wherever they went, he went with them. It was this Presence that constituted them a people, distinct from all other peoples. They were the people of the Presence.

In the community of faith there ought not to be any artificial separation between the sacred and the secular. Elevated language is used to describe the craftsmen who designed and built the tabernacle. Of Bezalel it is said that he was filled with the Spirit of God, with ability and intelligence, with knowledge and all craftsmanship (31:3). It took the dedicated work of men like Bezalel to bring the tabernacle to completion. And it took the gifts of all the Israelites to make the work possible.

All work undertaken for the glory of God is sacred in his sight. In every age pastors and lay people need to work together hand in hand for the glory of God. In God's sight the work of both is equally important and equally sacred. The whole of life should reflect the reality of God's presence. It gives meaning to all of human existence.

The life of God's people is nourished and sustained by specific acts of worship through which the living reality of God's presence is repeatedly affirmed. God's presence for Israel was actualized through the experience of worship. Because of this fact Israel attached much importance to the sabbath at the *time* for worship (Ex. 31:12-17; 35:1-3) and to the tabernacle as the *place* for worship. We do not have detailed information about the services held at the sanctuary, but we do know that it was designated as the center of worship for the community. One of the names by which it is sometimes called is "the tent of meeting" (40:32).[9] However, it was not simply, nor even primarily, a place where people met together. Rather, it was the place where Israel met with God. It was the perpetual symbol of his continuing presence in their midst.

God's presence with his pilgrim people in the wilderness is a promise of his presence with us. The time of wilderness wanderings was a learning experience for Israel. Even after she entered Canaan, she continued to think of herself as a pilgrim people. No earthly city, no political state, no human achievement could satisfy her deepest needs. Through this experience she learned that man does not live by bread alone, but by the life-giving Word of God. Above all else, she learned that her true destiny was to be a holy people living in fellowship with the holy God (19:4-6).

We are faced today with a retreat from settled life and a return to nomadic living. A great part of mankind has been uprooted from familiar surroundings and thrust out into the wilderness. A new breed of nomads wanders over the face of the earth. These are the migrant workers, the war refugees, the military personnel, the hard-core unemployed, and the job transferees.

No one knows yet how we will adapt to this new nomadism. Does Exodus have anything to say to our situation? If so, will we be willing to listen? Will we be judged as the generation that concluded that God was indeed dead? Or will we, like Israel of old, discover afresh the presence of God even in the midst of our wilderness wanderings? Will we walk with God, or will we choose to walk alone? The God of the road awaits our response.

Personal Learning Activities

1. Arrange by alphabetical listing (*a,b,c,* etc.) the following events in their proper chronology:
   ____ (1) Moses saw the golden calf (32:19).
   ____ (2) Israel departed Egypt (13:2-6,17-18).
   ____ (3) Moses reascended Mount Sinai (34:27-28).
   ____ (4) Israel arrived at Mount Sinai (19:1).
   ____ (5) The covenant-making ceremony took place (19:16).
   ____ (6) Moses ascended Sinai the first time and was given the law, as well as tabernacle and worship instructions (24:12 to 31:18).
   ____ (7) The covenant was renewed and Moses was given the law a second time on Sinai (34:27-28).
   ____ (8) Moses broke tables of law (32:19).

2. The tabernacle provisions were given Israel to solve a theological problem. From the statements below select and mark that statement which best explains the problem:
   ____ (1) Moses was afraid.
   ____ (2) The gods of other nations were identified with a particular place.
   ____ (3) Moses and Israel needed assurance of the covenant-presence as they journeyed to Canaan.

3. In Exodus 33:12-23 Moses made three requests of God. Match request and response by placing letter by numerals:
   ____ (1) Moses asked for a guide. ____ (a) Moses saw God's glory after it passed.
   ____ (2) Moses asked for God's presence. ____ (b) Hobab was enlisted.
   ____ (3) Moses asked to see God's glory. ____ (c) Instructions for the tabernacle were given.

4. Place the tabernacle items listed below on the diagram. Match the letter to the number:
   ____ (1) Ark of the covenant.
   ____ (2) Holy of holies.
   ____ (3) Altar of incense.
   ____ (4) Golden candlestick.
   ____ (5) Table of divine presence.
   ____ (6) Laver.
   ____ (7) Altar of burnt offering.

5. Review the section "Lessons for Life from the Scriptures." Which truth is most meaningful to you, and why?

---

[1]Walter Zimmerli, "Promise and Fulfillment," in *Essays on Old Testament Hermeneutics,* ed. Claus Westermann, trans. James Luther Mays (Richmond: John Knox Press, 1964), p. 109.

[2]Buber, *op. cit.,* p. 42.

[3]Martin Noth, *Exodus,* trans. J.S. Bowden (Philadelphia: The Westminster Press, 1962), p. 253.

[4]W.B.J. Martin, "The Unrecognized God," *The Expository Times,* Nov. 1965 (Vol. LXXVII), p. 53.

[5]For a detailed description of the tabernacle and its furnishings, see G. Henton Davies, "Tabernacle," *The Interpreter's Dictionary of the Bible,* ed. George Arthur Buttrick, Vol. 4 (Nashville: Abingdon Press, 1962), pp. 498-506.

[6]R.B.Y. Scott, "Weights, Measures, Money and Time," in *Peake's Commentary on the Bible,* ed. Matthew Black and H.H. Rowley (London: Thomas Nelson and Sons, Ltd., 1962), pp. 37-41.

[7]Hyatt, *op. cit.,* pp. 288-89.

[8]J. Edgar Park, "Exodus," *The Interpreter's Bible,* ed. George Arthur Buttrick, Vol. 1 (Nashville: Abingdon Press, 1952), pp. 1038-39.

[9]The use of the phrase "tent of meeting" in 40:32 is in reference to the tabernacle. The same phrase in 33:7 refers to the site used by Moses prior to the tabernacle.

THE CHURCH STUDY COURSE

The Church Study Course consists of a variety of short-term credit courses for adults and youth and noncredit foundational units for children and preschoolers. The materials are for use in addition to the study and training curriculums made available to the churches on an ongoing basis.

Study courses and foundational units are organized into a system that is promoted by the Sunday School Board, 127 Ninth Avenue, North, Nashville, Tennessee 37234, by the Woman's Missionary Union, 600 North Twentieth Street, Birmingham, Alabama 35203; by the Brotherhood Commission, 1548 Poplar Avenue, Memphis, Tennessee 38104; and by the respective departments of the state conventions affiliated with the Southern Baptist Convention.

Study course materials are flexible enough to be adapted to the needs of any Baptist church. The resources are published in several different formats—textbooks of various sizes, workbooks, and kits. Each item contains a brief explanation of the Church Study Course and information on requesting credit. Additional information and interpretation are available from the participating agencies.

Types of Study and Credit

Adults and youth can earn study course credit through individual or group study. Teachers of courses or of foundational units also are eligible to receive credit.

1. Class Experience.—Group involvement with course material for the designated number of hours for the particular course.
   A person who is absent from one or more sessions must complete the "Personal Learning Activities" or other requirements for the course.
2. Individual Study.—This includes reading, viewing, or listening to course material and completing the specified requirements for the course.
3. Lesson Course Study.—Parallel use of designated study course material during the study of selected units in Church Program Organization periodical curriculum units. Guidance for this means of credit appears in the selected periodical.
4. Institutional Study.—Parallel use of designated study course material during regular courses at educational institutions, including Seminary Extension Department courses. Guidance for this means of credit is provided by the teacher.

Credit is awarded for the successful completion of a course of study. This credit is granted by the Church Study Course Awards Office, 127 Ninth Avenue, North, Nashville, Tennessee 37234, for the participating agencies. Form 151 (available free) is recommended for use in requesting credit.

When credit is issued to a person on request, the Awards Office sends two copies of a notice of credit earned to the church. The original copy of the credit slip should be filed by the study course clerk in the participant's record of training folder. The duplicate should be given to the person who earned the credit. Accumulated credits are applied toward leadership or member development diplomas, which are measures of learning, growth, development, and training.

Detailed information about the Church Study Course system of credits, diplomas, and record keeping is available from the participating agencies. Study course materials, supplementary teaching or learning aids, and forms for record keeping may be ordered from Baptist Book Stores.

The Church Study Course Curriculum

Credit is granted on those courses listed in the current copy of *Church Services and Materials Catalog* and *Baptist Book Store Catalog*. When selecting couses or foundational units, check the current catalogs to determine what study course materials are valid.

How to Request Credit for This Course

This book is the text for a course in the subject area Bible Studies.

This course is designed for 6 hours of group study. Credit is awarded for satisfactory class experience with the study material for the minimum number of hours. A person who is absent from one or more sessions must complete the "Personal Learning Activities" or other requirements for the materials missed.

Credit is also allowed for use of this material in individual study and in institutional study, if so designated.

The following requirements must be met for credit in this course:
1. Read the book *Exodus: Called for Redemptive Mission*.
2. Attend at least 6 hours of class study or complete all "Personal Learning Activities" (see end of each chapter). A class member who is absent from one or more class sessions must complete "Personal Learning Activities" on chapters missed. In such a case, he must turn in his paper by the date the teacher sets, usually within ten days following the last class.

Credit in this course may be earned through individual study. The requirements for such credit are:
1. Read the book.
2. Complete the "Personal Learning Activities" on the chapters.
Credit in this course may be earned through study in an educational institution, if so designated by a teacher. The requirements are:
1. Read the book.
2. Fulfill the requirements of the course taught at the institution.
After the course is completed, the teacher, the study course records librarian, the learner, or any person designated by the church should complete Form 151 ("Church Study Course Credit Request, Revised 1975") and send it to the Awards Office, 127 Ninth Avenue, North, Nashville, Tennessee 37234. In the back of this book the reader will find a form which he may cut out, fill in, and send to the Awards Office.

Cut along this line

INSTRUCTIONS: If requested by the teacher, fill in this form and give it to him when the course is completed. If preferred, mail this request for course credit to

AWARDS OFFICE
THE SUNDAY SCHOOL BOARD, SBC
127 NINTH AVENUE, NORTH
NASHVILLE, TENNESSEE 37234

State Convention	Association		Indicate Type of Study (X)	
			☐ Class ☐ Individual	☐ Lesson Course ☐ Educational Institution

CHURCH

Church Name

Mailing Address

City, State, Zip Code

MAIL TO

Mail to (If Different from Church Address)

Street, Route, or P.O. Box

City, State, Zip Code

LAST NAME	FIRST NAME AND MIDDLE INITIAL	MRS. (X)	COURSE TITLE			
			Exodus: Called for Redemptive Mission			